Praise fo...
Under a Wing

"A lyrical memoir."

—*People*

"A lovely evocation of the mixed feelings any child has for a parent, with equal parts love, resentment, fear and belonging."

—James Tobin, *Chicago Tribune*

"Resonates with intimate detail . . . restoring the humanity behind the fame."

—Bob Thompson, *The Washington Post*

"[A] touching memoir."

—Benjamin Schwarz, *Los Angeles Times*

"An elegant domestic tale . . . the private story of a family whose members were as intimately linked with American history as they were with one another—and the inner workings of the human heart."

—Susan Cheever, *USA Today*

"Lindbergh's youngest has written an evocative reminiscence of her youth. This gentle memoir shows a unique and uniquely poignant family life."

—*Publishers Weekly*

"A sweetly moving memoir. . . . An eloquent recollection of a happy childhood in a tightly-knit family whose parents' celebrity complicated but did not contort their lives."

—*Kirkus Reviews*

Under a Wing

* A Memoir

Reeve Lindbergh

Simon & Schuster Paperbacks
New York   London   Toronto   Sydney

Simon & Schuster Paperbacks
A Division of Simon & Schuster, Inc.
1230 Avenue of the Americas
New York, NY 10020

This Simon & Schuster trade paperback edition May 2009

SIMON & SCHUSTER PAPERBACKS and colophon are
registered trademarks of Simon & Schuster, Inc.

For information about special discounts for bulk purchases,
please contact Simon & Schuster Special Sales at
1-800-456-6798 or business@simonandschuster.com.

Designed by Karolina Harris

Manufactured in the United States of America

10 9 8 7 6 5 4 3 2 1

Library of Congress Cataloging-in-Publication Data is available.

ISBN-13: 978-1-4391-4883-9
ISBN-10:   1-4391-4883-X

Grateful acknowledgment is made to the following for permission to re-
print from the works mentioned:

    Harcourt, Brace, Jovanovich for *Hour of Gold, Hour of Lead: Diaries and
Letters of Anne Morrow Lindbergh*, 1929–1932 by Anne Morrow Lindbergh,
copyright © 1973 by Harcourt, Brace, Jovanovich; *Earth Shrine* by Anne
Morrow Lindbergh, copyright © 1969 by Harcourt, Brace & World; and
North to the Orient by Anne Morrow Lindbergh, copyright 1935 by Har-
court, Brace & Co.

    Alfred A. Knopf for *Beast, Bird and Fish* by Elizabeth Cutter Morrow,
copyright 1933 by Alfred A. Knopf.

    Pantheon Books for *Gift from the Sea* by Anne Morrow Lindbergh,
copyright 1955 by Pantheon Books, and *The Unicorn and Other Poems* by
Anne Morrow Lindbergh, copyright 1956 by Pantheon Books.

Photo Credits
Courtesy of the author: 3, 16–18, 20; courtesy of Richard Brown: 19;
The Lindbergh Collection, Sterling Memorial Library, Yale University:
4–15; Minnesota Historical Society: 1–2.

✳ *Acknowledgments*

M A N Y people have helped me with this book, but a lot
of them probably don't know it. I am grateful to my closest
family members for their support, their candor, and their courage. To my mother, Anne Morrow Lindbergh, I owe the impulse to write and the instruction to "tell one's own truth," as a
writer, wherever the telling may lead. To my three brothers and
to my late sister, I am so grateful for honesty, insight, affection,
and for detailed memories more accurate than my own. Thanks
to my daughters, Elizabeth and Susannah Brown, for encourag-
ing my work consistently and for putting up with my literary
preoccupations, and to my son Benjamin for his ability to cheer
me up under any circumstances. I thank Ned Perrin, my sister's
husband, and Constance Feydy and Marek Sapieyevski, my
sister's children, for the great gift of their closeness in my life,
especially during the time spent working on this book. Above
all, thanks to my beloved husband, Nathaniel Tripp, for his
compassionate patience and thoughtful listening over the
years. (I thank his sons Eli and Sam Tripp for showing those
very same qualities, and I thank his mother, Alice Tripp, for
her humor, tenacity, and inimitable style, all of which have
heartened me during this period.)

Thanks also to other family members for their thoughts,

occasional tactful corrections, and valuable contributions: Margot Wilkie and her daughters, Faith Morrow Williams and Constance Morrow Fulenwider, as well as my "Morgan cousins," Saran Hutchins, Elisabeth Pendleton, Rhidian Morgan, and Eiluned Morgan.

Thanks to Jim and Ellie Newton for their memories and for their influence, in both my writing and my heart, for more than fifty years. Thanks to Richard Brown and his family for their lasting affection and kindness, and to Marie Arana-Ward and A. Scott Berg for their friendship as well as their wisdom.

Special thanks to the "End of the Road Writers Group" in Vermont for suffering with me through the first drafts of the book. Thanks to Colonel Raymond Fredette, David McCullough, T. Willard Hunter, Elsie Mayer, Roxanne Chadwick, Anne Johnson, Ev Cassagneres, and David Kirk Vaughan, for work that has been particularly helpful to me. Thanks also to Don Westfall and his staff at the Lindbergh Home and Historical Site, to the people of Little Falls, and to the Minnesota Historical Society for welcoming our family so warmly into our own history in the years since my father's death. Thanks to the North Haven Historical Society and the winter and summer residents of North Haven, Maine, to Judith Schiff and the Sterling Memorial Library at Yale University, to The Missouri Historical Society in St. Louis, to the Smith College Archives, Amherst College, Princeton University, The Smithsonian Air and Space Museum, and the Charles A. and Anne Morrow Lindbergh Foundation for valuable information and research assistance.

Finally, thanks to my agent and good friend, Rhoda Weyr, for sticking with this writer for so long in spite of "my mud and my cows," and to Rebecca Saletan, Bob Bender, Jackie Seow, Johanna Li, Fred Chase, Gypsy da Silva, and all at Simon & Schuster for your wonderful assistance and encouragement.

*For my brothers, Jon, Land, and Scott
with love and thanks always*

✳ Contents

1

Imagining the Lindberghs

✳ IN kindergarten, one of my brothers told a friend on the playground that our father had discovered America. At about the same age, I dreamed that he was God. The relief brought by that revelation shone upon me the next morning like the bright rays of dawn. If our father was God, it explained everything: why we called him "Father," when all of our friends called their fathers "Daddy"; why he had so little contact with the other families around us, and yet so many people spoke about him with a kind of reverence; why we had to eat Pepperidge Farm bread at home rather than Wonder Bread; why the house shook when he was in a bad mood; and why I could find him in the *Encyclopaedia Britannica.*

I am the youngest child and second daughter of Charles A. and Anne Morrow Lindbergh. My father, Charles Augustus Lindbergh, became internationally famous in May 1927 for making the first nonstop solo flight from New York to Paris, in a single-engine Ryan monoplane called the *Spirit of St. Louis.* He was twenty-five years old. My mother, Anne Morrow, met him in December of the following year when he made a good-will trip to Mexico, where her father was serving as the American ambassador. She was twenty-two. They were married in

1929 and lived together for more than forty years until his death in 1974.

As fliers, my mother and father explored the world together, mapping air routes for the aviation industry in its infancy. As writers, they published many accounts of their adventures and their thoughts. His best-known volume was *The Spirit of St. Louis,* describing the 1927 flight. Hers was *Gift from the Sea,* a philosophical meditation on women's lives in this century.

When they were young parents, close to the beginning of their marriage, my father and mother suffered the death of their first child, Charles, as the result of a highly publicized kidnapping. My mother was pregnant at the time with her second son, my brother Jon. After Jon was born, my parents retreated from public life in order to raise him, and then the rest of their children, in protective privacy. They moved many times before I was born, seeking quiet and avoiding the press. They lived in England, in France, in Michigan, on Long Island, New York, and finally, just after the Second World War, bought the house in Darien, Connecticut, on the shores of Long Island Sound, where I grew up. Over the years they became so successful at this effort to remove their family from the public eye that many people are unaware that there were more Lindbergh children after that first, lost baby whose story was so well known, and whose brothers and sisters never knew him at all.

In fact, there were five of us: Jon, Land, Anne, Scott, and Reeve, three sons and two daughters. We grew up as the children of celebrities, but because our parents worked so hard to remove themselves from celebrity life, our understanding of what that meant was fluid and imperfect. It remains uncertain and idiosyncratic even today. We Lindberghs still know ourselves best as a tribe: close-knit, self-enclosed, and self-defining, always prepared to be besieged by invisible forces upwelling from the past: the famous flight, the kidnapping, the controversy over our father's isolationist stance just before the Second World War.

Although it is now more than twenty years since he died, we are still directed and dominated by our father's strength of character. Although she is more than ninety years old, often confused in her mind, and in fragile health at this writing, we are still redeemed, gentled, and sustained by our mother.

"Was I married?" she will ask me, her eyes wide with astonishment at the thought. Or, "Are you my sister?" But when my own sister, her other daughter, Anne, was dying, and I could do nothing to help Anne, could not stop the process, I put my arms around our mother and cried because I thought my heart was breaking, and also because I thought that she, my greatest comfort all my life, was now too disoriented even to understand what was going on. But my mother embraced me in return, and she wept, too, in her flannel nightgown with the pink rosebuds on it, and she patted my head and then said exactly the right thing.

"You never did anything wrong, Reeve. You never did anything wrong."

In our family it has always been hard to know what is right and what is wrong, in terms of what we can do for one another. It has been hard for us, too, to separate individual identity from family identity. As the youngest, I imagined growing up by virtue of a succession of transformations, becoming first one member of my family and then another until I had been handed benevolently all the way up the line into adulthood. By the time I was twelve I would have my brother Scott's forgetfulness, his bashful grace, and his ability to befriend snakes and turtles. At fifteen I would be Anne, with straight blond hair and a blue-and-white-checked bikini, small-featured and arrestingly lovely to look at, playing her flute with fingertips faintly scented by the oranges that came to us in crates from Florida once a month, which Anne peeled and ate, one after another, all day long. Later on I would be Land, a cowboy and a cattleman, and then Jon, with mask and tanks and flippers, exploring the sea.

Beyond Jon there were only my parents. In trying to imagine who they were, entertaining the possibilities of who I could become through them, my images of entitled reincarnation blurred and became much vaguer, more diffuse, and thoroughly improbable. My sources for these imaginings ranged from the tabloids to my favorite fairy tales, and with their help I could blend my parents' legendary inaccessible accomplishments with my own fantasies: rescuing people from burning buildings, being President, being Peter Pan, flying without wings.

We were not a typical 1950s suburban family. We never owned a television set during my father's lifetime, we did not attend church or belong to any community organizations, we were not allowed to eat candy or read comic books in the house, and when a biographer asked me recently whether my father knew who Elvis Presley was, I could not tell him, not for sure.

I would quite often find pictures of my father in books and magazines when I was growing up, and I would recognize him at once, even though the photographs invariably showed him as a young man in a flying helmet, and had been taken almost twenty years before I was born. All the same, the boy flier belonged to our family, I knew that. His eyes and nose, cheek and chin, his life and his story were unmistakably ours. If he was not exactly the father I knew, then he was like another older brother, living forever in the same image, in a life that did not touch but still ran parallel to my own. When I look at these photographs today, I react in the same way. This face is familiar, and familial. It is part of me and what is mine, but it is also distant and inert. It will not move or speak. This face will remain stuck in its historical context like a fly in amber, where it belongs.

Once in a while, though, I come across a photograph of my father from my own childhood era, not the slim young man in the flying suit but someone older, grayer, and heavier, with thinning hair. He is standing with a group of airline officials, perhaps, or among scientists at Bethesda Naval Hospital. He is wearing his navy blue pinstripe suit, and is in his conversational stance. His head is slightly tilted for listening, partly because he is deaf in one ear from the engines of early airplanes, although he won't admit it, and partly because at six foot two inches he is accustomed to talking with people who are not as tall as he is. His weight is off one foot, so he can rock back infinitesimally on the other. He is a shy, courteous man who will not inflict nervous agitation on himself or other people, but he is generally more comfortable in some degree of motion. His right arm is crooked at the elbow and his right hand forms a loose fist, thumb pointed up.

I am sure he is about to say something to his colleagues, and that he will begin with some cautious phrase like, "I think we have to remember . . ." He will then punctuate his statement with a quick emphatic jerk of that thumb, as some might point a forefinger, to make his point. I am not at all sure, though, that he is going to stay on the page, the way the boy aviator does. This man really is my father, after all, and he might walk right out of history and into his family life again, as he has done so many times before. He might walk across the gravel driveway, down the stone path, and through the arched front doorway of the old house in Connecticut where the rest of us are waiting, and then he will close the door behind him.

2 At Home

✳ FOR many people, I think, the words "family structure" connote some abstract concept like "nuclear family" or "family tree." For me, however, the family structure was also a real place—the old stone house in Connecticut, which contained and structured my whole Lindbergh family life.

From the inside, the door seemed enormous, medieval, and so heavy it should creak. It was made of varnished and deeply paneled golden oak, six inches thick, and its openings and shuttings carried all the importance that weight conveys. The arched shape and the golden color made it look to me like a giant Gothic waffle, set in stone. It was because of the odd shape, I suppose, that there was not even the seasonal relief of a screen door, to reverberate with the casual spring and slam of lighthearted living. Summer or winter, going in or out through our front door was something to be taken seriously.

The door opened into a small square entryway that I remember as a cool cave of stone, with a window in one of its walls letting in a little light and giving a view of a rocky outcropping, a tangle of low foliage, and the trunk and lower branches of a big oak tree in the background. There was a foot scraper, as well as a rough and bristly mat, just outside the doorway, and another mat just inside, for wiping off any residue of gravel from the driveway or mud from the cove that might be tracked in on our sneakers or our boots or even our bare feet. We didn't often wear our shoes during the summertime.

I have always liked to go barefoot, and I have always liked my feet, and my hands too. There were a few adolescent years when this was not true, a period when I hated my hands and feet with a passion, along with my nose and my hair, my height and especially my rear end. (Even though I hardly ever saw it, and only by twisting my head around in awkward positions to catch a glimpse in the mirror, it offended me.) But generally, throughout my life, I have felt strong affection for all the hands and feet in my family, mine included. They are not beautiful, perhaps, by other people's standards, but they are singular, and they link us unmistakably as Lindberghs.

I could pick out my siblings anywhere, however well disguised they might be otherwise, given just one good look at their naked fingers and toes: agile, strong, bony, and freckled, with visible blue veins and with baggy wrinkles around the knuckles. We look as though somebody made a mistake when designing our hands and ordered the skin two sizes bigger than the bones. We also have too-small, flat fingernails, and toenails that grow in the wrong direction, not demurely out and down, as in an advertisement for fingernail polish, but eccentrically out and up, in a way that threatens to curl over backwards like a Turkish slipper if allowed to grow unchecked.

I loved my bare feet and was proud of the leathery callused soles I developed each year by walking all over the property without shoes, beginning as soon as school let out for the summer. It took a couple of weeks at first before I could cross the gravel driveway without wincing, and no bare foot was proof against piercing by a stray piece of glass in the woods or slicing by a live oyster shell hiding in the blue-black sucking mud of Scott's Cove, a more likely injury. Our father was so vigilant about outdoor dangers of every magnitude, large or small, that we had almost no broken glass on the property. We didn't have rusty nails, either, or barbed wire, or even poison ivy. As long as he was responsible for it, his children were safe to walk, free from fear or footgear, anywhere on his land. We just had to wipe our feet afterward.

Outside our door, along with the doormat and foot scraper, there was a witch. She was always there, whenever I went in or out, day or night. She did not ride a broom, but instead stood like a sentinel in her pointed hat and flaring skirt on an elaborate series of black metal curls and curlicues mounted against the stone foundation to the right of the archway, much higher than my head. This witch was painted black all over, and hanging from her skirt like a long, thick, loose thread there was a black metal wire for visitors to pull. She was a bell. We were not encouraged to pull the wire, though, as we were told that she was an antique, and very fragile. Her demeanor was so stiff and proper that I was not tempted to ring her bell anyway. It would have been an indignity.

Inside the house, directly facing the door through which we entered, there was a coat closet as wide as the entryway itself. Here we shed our outer clothing along with our outdoor and our nonfamily selves, immediately upon entering the house.

In this coat closet there hung a black velvet evening coat belonging to my mother, with velvet buttons extending from collar to hem, as well as a series of pink perfumed raincoats she wore into New York City. In the pockets of these, along with an occasional favorite horse chestnut, or folded handker-chief, or worn emery board, she kept accordion-pleated strips of transparent plastic that looked and felt like something she had forgotten to throw away. They seemed to be nothing more than limp and crumpled bits of used wax paper, but they were instead collapsible rain hats that she saved in her pockets from year to year. They could be unfolded in a sudden New York City shower to tie carefully under her chin, and they would protect her head without flattening her coiffure after she had been to the hairdresser, or when she was going to have tea with a friend at the Cosmopolitan Club, or to shop at Best & Co. or Bloomingdale's.

For us children, in the family closet, there were waist-length zippered jackets, and snowsuits with suspenders, and red, yellow, or green rain slickers hanging on hooks by their shiny hoods, and serviceably warm winter coats and parkas that had not yet, in the 1950s, bloomed into the light, multicolored, thickly down-filled garments of today. There were the hip-length mud boots, so tall that they flopped over on themselves, that Jon wore for mucking in the Sound and digging for clams at low tide. There were ice skates and mittens and scarves and hats, an occasional hockey stick, and in my teens a camel hair coat exactly like the ones all of my friends wore (I hoped), with deep pockets and a belt across the back. During Anne's college years, she would come home on weekends and hang up in this closet a voluminous, fuzzy, cocoonlike winter coat that dominated all the other clothes like a peacock in a chicken yard, and was a shade of purple which she and our mother referred to as "aubergine." I associated the romantic sound of the French syllables with Aubusson carpets and Almay perfumes, and felt both deceived and disgusted when I learned that the word only meant "eggplant."

Hanging in this closet, too, was my father's heavy military overcoat, which may have been part of his Air Force uniform, but which I never saw him wear at home, alongside the familiar, worn, light tan leather jacket he used when he was working at the far end of our driveway on fall afternoons, sawing, splitting, or chopping wood. He would do this near the rhododendrons by his sawhorses and the green, asbestos-shingled doghouse that no dog ever wanted to live in. There was also a navy zippered windbreaker he wore in fall and spring on the water, and an enormous, knee-length, khaki-colored parka with a fur-lined hood, perhaps a relic of the polar flights over Greenland to Asia with my mother, in the 1930s.

In this parka he looked taller than ever, and even more determinedly adapted to adversity, a combination of Admiral Byrd and some intense, elongated Eskimo elder. He only wore it on rare, very cold days, when the cove was frozen over with flaky, cloud-colored saltwater ice, and the temperature of the air numbed my mittened fingers the minute I stepped outside, and my nostrils stuck together with every breath.

My father treated his fur-lined-parka days with a profound respect, bordering on reverence, for cold weather. When he wore this coat we heard about the subzero Minnesota winters of his own childhood, about the virtues of wood stoves, kerosene lanterns, and Hudson Bay blankets, and about farmers who had perished between house and barn trying to make their way to their cows through depths of blinding snow. Or we would learn from him a lesson that I remember today as the Seven Signs of Frostbite, though I may have mixed it up with the Seven Dwarfs, in Disney's cartoon fantasy *Snow White* of the same era, because his teaching remains in my mind now as three words used to describe frostbitten skin: "Waxy, Pale, and Hard," to which I instinctively want to add, "Sleepy, Sneezy, Grumpy, and Dopey."

Our father was full-hearted about extreme conditions, especially of weather. He eagerly—but never, he would remind us, foolishly—awaited the thunderstorms, floods, and blizzards that frightened other people, the ones that were heralded by urgent warnings on local radio stations, and accompanied by panicked flockings to area grocery stores. My father instead checked the thermometers, scanned the skies, roamed the property in his parka, and kept the household ever alert, informed, and prepared. He had on hand emergency food and water, flashlights, extra blankets, medical equipment, rubber rafts, snakebite kits, and even a vial of morphine, which was probably illegal. We could have withstood famine, flood, plague, siege, and possibly even nuclear war, thanks to our father, and he rarely let us forget it. We had to be prepared, he told us. We had to be ready for anything. He was ever on the alert for dangers, although the dangers were unspecified.

"It's the unforeseen . . ." he would warn us, "it's always the unforeseen. . . ." His eyes were alight with purpose, his voice resonated with the rich and distant timbre of experience.

There were few dangers in the Connecticut of my early childhood, as far as I could tell. There were acres of open fields near us, and deep, brambly woods that stretched without apparent limit on all sides except where the houses, or the shoreline, held them back. Sleeping Beauty thickets of brambles and vines grew in profuse, obscuring tangles between our house and the road, and between the house and the water. This was wilderness by design, rather than neglect. My father cleared the brush, and chopped down and sawed up and split the felled trees and branches for the fire, but he always left enough of the woods alone so that from a boat in the cove, or from a car passing by on the road beyond our driveway, it would have been almost impossible to learn anything about our lives.

There were stretches of mud and marsh grass along the shore, and stands of tall cattails crowded the roadsides. On autumn weekends duck hunters concealed themselves among the cattails on low-slung motorboats, their presence betrayed when the wind shifted by the shine of green Evinrude motors, weighing down the sterns, like oily overgrown dragonflies.

The hunters were not supposed to come near the houses. Once I saw a boat and two men with shotguns lurking in our own marsh grass, and ran back home to tell my father, every running step loaded with excitement and a sense of mission. Potential invasion was one of the few things that could legitimately be used to rouse our father from his office, where he spent most of the time when he was at home, if he was not working outdoors.

I knew that rousing him was a good idea. My father, when roused, was always interesting, and besides, I felt sorry for the ducks. Was it not Eleanor Roosevelt herself who had cautioned us to be kind to our web-footed friends? Our mother had taught Anne and me the song associated with the former First Lady, and we would all sing it together, our mother laughing until she cried and had to blow her nose, as Anne and I puffed out our chests and spread out our arms like the opera singers in Bugs Bunny cartoons, affecting the throaty, flat-voweled and hollow accents we thought most appropriate to presidential families, radio performances, and the ASPCA:

> *Be kind to your web-footed friends.*
> *Every duck may be somebody's muhhhther,*
> *Be kind to your friends in the swump*
> *Where the weath-ah is cold and dump.*
> *Now you may think that this is the end . . .*
> *Well, it is!*

When our ducks were in actual danger, I had no time to sing. Instead I ran to find my father. I knocked respectfully on his office door, and I said in a polite, breathless, but nonetheless intent voice the words that always opened his door: "Father? Somebody is *on our property!*"

He stopped typing right away, as I knew he would, and he

scraped back his chair from the desk and opened the door to me, grim-faced and purposeful, demanding details. Then he told me to stay in the house, and he strode off in the direction of the marsh, tall as a giant and already darkening like a thunderstorm by the time he walked through the front door.

I don't know what my father said to the duck hunters when he found them, but by the time he came back to the house again I could just barely hear the sputtering putt of the Evinrude moving farther and farther away across the cove, until finally it had disappeared.

He had both the easy confidence and the electrically charged manner of a person who has often lived with emergency: on the farm, in the air, and in time of war. He was calmest in practical crisis, and grew most restless during quiet periods. I sometimes felt sorry for him when there weren't any emergencies in our neighborhood. When the floods and blizzards were all threatening other families, and the sun was shining over our own heads day after day in a blue and cloudless sky, what was my father to do with himself? But I knew that bad weather would someday return, and then we could all be comfortable again. My father would stride out to meet the hurricane, flood, or blizzard, wearing his fur-lined parka and carrying within him a kind of jubilation.

3
Punk Design

✳ I LOVED each and every piece of equipment that accompanied our father's philosophy of preparedness. I have always had a fascination for anything collapsible, reversible, or transitional in nature. There were so many wonderful things in our household: umbrellas and pup tents, kaleidoscopes and camp stools, the limp-looking, mud-colored square of rubber tarpaulin kept on a shelf in my father's closet, which transformed itself before my very eyes into an air mattress when he took it out and blew into the little tube tucked into one of its corners. My father's cheeks would puff out and his forehead would furrow with effort while he breathed a comical, lopsided buoyancy into the mattress, and it came to life like a reluctant, drunken magic carpet. Then, in summertime, whoever wanted to do so could bring a sleeping bag and place it, and him- or herself, with the greatest possible care, on top of the inflated mattress (there could be no kneeling, bouncing, or bringing sharp objects on board: this was not a pool toy; this was a very serious piece of equipment), and sleep out under the stars, or in a pup tent, or even on my parents' screened porch, which extended far beyond their second-floor bedroom of the old house in Darien, almost into the branches of the big pine tree by the window.

Rolled up in a sleeping bag, floating on the air mattress with even the sharpness of my elbows tucked in to avoid inflicting damage, I thought this was like sleeping in heaven. I was up off the ground, and literally airborne, but still surrounded by my whole family, and still within earshot of the seagulls' crying as they wheeled over our cove, and the katydids throbbing steadily into the humid August nights of Long Island Sound.

Along with the air mattress, my father had a number of other possessions that I thought enchantingly intricate: a Swiss Army knife, retractable measuring tapes, a shaving kit that he could take apart completely and would put away, when he finished shaving, down at the bottom of a sock (knotted at the ankle to keep its component parts from rattling in his briefcase when he traveled). He also had a normal-looking flashlight with an ugly hexagonal head, to which feature he drew our attention every time he put the flashlight down on a flat surface.

"You see that?" He would point. "It doesn't move." We saw. The flashlight lay there on the shelf, or the table, or the floor, exactly as he had placed it. It didn't move a bit. Nor did we, as he fixed us with his penetrating, instructive blue eyes.

"It doesn't roll off the table," he would say, looking at us searchingly, challenging someone to contradict him. Nobody did.

"Why aren't all flashlights made like this one?" he wondered aloud. None of us would hazard a guess.

"Cylinders!" He explained irritably. "You buy a flashlight, nine times out of ten it comes in a cylindrical shape. Now, a cylinder will always roll. A cylinder was *made* to roll. And rolling is fine, for a rolling pin. But you put down a cylindrical flashlight in the dark, near a place where you're working, so you can use two hands, and what's it going to do? It's going to roll away from you, of course! Off the shelf, under the car . . . what good is that?"

No good at all, we knew. And we knew what he would say next, too.

"All they would have to do is change the shape of the head. Not the whole flashlight, just the head. The whole problem would be solved. What's the matter with these people? Pentagonal, hexagonal, even a square, for heaven's sake. Just the head. . . ."

He would shake his own head in frustration, lamenting the shortsightedness of invisible engineers. He warned us all during the course of our lives with him about the evils of what he called "punk design," a creeping and generalized shoddiness of plan which was infecting too many aspects of modern life, and compromising the excellence of too many modern products, including all cylindrical flashlights and more than a few automobiles.

My father had especially high standards where automobiles were concerned. He impressed upon us the fact that a car, especially one that was poorly designed or poorly handled, was just as dangerous as a revolver. His familiarity with and respect for all kinds of machines being wide-ranging and profound, he expressed his feelings about them in a grimly fatalistic way to each new driver in the family.

"The machine," he would say with dire emphasis, "never forgives." He would mitigate the statement by assuring us that our mother and father would *always* forgive us, no matter how foolish or how disastrous our mistakes might be. Our friends would no doubt forgive us, too. God, even, might well forgive us our trespasses and our poor judgments and all the personal "punk designs" of our lives. But a machine, my father told us, hammering in this point many, many times, would not. A machine could give neither absolution nor even a second chance. One mistake, to many machines, was a capital offense.

This kind of thinking, coupled with a respect for fuel economy that came from his aviation career—wasted fuel meant shorter distances traveled, whether for the pilot of the *Spirit of St. Louis* or for a group of World War II fighters in the Pacific —caused our father to drive at fifty-five miles per hour on the Connecticut highways long before the OPEC oil crisis made it a common practice. As teenagers, we gritted our teeth with frustration and envy as other drivers sped by our family's Ford station wagons or VW Bugs, in their flashy Corvettes and Karmann Ghias whipping along at sixty-five or seventy miles per hour through Stamford and Old Greenwich and Cos Cob, while our father persisted, unperturbed as the turtle in Aesop's fable. He courteously pulled over into the far right lane to make way for the speeders, and he firmly kept two hands on the steering wheel at all times. ("Think of it as a clock, Reeve. Put your left hand at ten o'clock and your right hand at two o'clock. Use an even grip, not too tight. Some people prefer nine o'clock and three o'clock, but I believe that ten and two will give you better control in most situations.") My father did not think that one could drive a car at sixty miles per hour, sixty-five, or higher, consistently over time, and achieve the same margin of safety and quality of fuel efficiency as at the official speed limit. Ultimately, by wearing down or by cracking up, the machine would not forgive.

An extension of this same philosophy kept him forever on the novice slopes of the ski areas to which he took his family for the long, healthy outdoor vacations he so approved in Vermont, or Canada, or later, Colorado, when we were growing up. The rest of the family, even our mother, took ski classes. We progressed from one level of skill to the next, taking our share of reckless chances and spectacular falls during our free skiing time. But our father never took a skiing lesson, just as he had never taken a sailing lesson, not at the time when he sailed with my mother's family in Maine, and not later, when he sailed with my mother and their close friend Jim Newton, through the Florida Keys, on the *Aldebaran,* a boat the three friends owned together. My father maintained that as long as he could grasp the basic principles of any sport, and was able to put these into practice, he was equipped with all that was necessary for safety and enjoyment, and this was all he cared about. He was interested neither in competition nor in speed, happy to sail a boat where he wanted it to go, and content to remain indefinitely the same slow, careful, deliberate skier, a warmly dressed figure who kept the top of his body bent forward at a certain angle so as to maintain his balance— always looking, on skis, like a tall man humbly preparing to go through a small door—and then snowplowed across the hill with his skis set in a 45 degree wedge, no more and no less, back and forth down the beginner's slope at the same pace and rhythm, all day.

We would ski down from the top of the mountain with our goggles and bright stocking caps and fat ski mitts and our flushed cheeks, and we would always find him there, traversing the hill among the novices and the little children, with his elbows in and his ski poles poked out behind him, stiff as two chicken wings. He always wore the same navy blue jacket and ski pants, the same navy blue hat—like a baseball cap, with a visor that stuck out in front but with flaps tied across the top that could be untied and pulled down to cover his ears in very cold weather. This looked to me like a subdued, rather military version of Elmer Fudd's hunting cap, in the Bugs Bunny cartoons. It made him look vulnerable and out of place among all the other brightly dressed people on the slopes, yet at the same time fully, perhaps even officially, committed to the task at hand. In this business of skiing healthily down the slope, my father looked as inexorable and as matter-of-fact as a daily mailman making his way through a snowstorm. It was not his job to be concerned with the fashions or the weather; he was intent only on completing his appointed rounds.

He never, ever fell down. We teased him about it, told him to relax, let himself go, and take a tumble now and then. It would make skiing much easier, we said. We might as well have saved our breath. He didn't want skiing to be easy. He liked it just the way it was. And besides, he told us, he didn't want to fall down. It went against nature, and it went against his training.

"In my profession," he explained, "you only fall once."

We were free to ski as we chose, and I am sure our father knew that we would someday drive as we chose, too, but while we lived with him, we were drilled in the particulars of handling ourselves and our automobiles as carefully as if we were a squadron of young fliers under his command, and he responsible for our survival. Long before we turned the ignition key in any car, we had to check the tires, the brakes, the lights, and the gas, oil, and water levels on our vehicles. Anywhere, at any time, we might be asked to stop and change a tire without advance warning. We were taken out deliberately to drive on icy roads, so that we became familiar with winter conditions and learned to "turn the wheel into a skid" if we hit a slippery patch. We learned to check the rear-view and the side-view mirrors, and to give a quick, over-the-shoulder backward glance out the driver's window before pulling over into the passing lane of traffic on the highway. We learned not to pull in again, after passing, until we could see both headlights of the car we had passed in our rear-view mirror again.

I have learned to appreciate many of the fine details of my

father's training, especially after having lived most of my adult life in places that require a lot of driving on icy roads. Still, my very favorite of all our father's warnings and instructions was a vague and all-encompassing, "And always, always, be sure to watch out for the *other* damn fool." Anne and I felt sure that this phrase referred to all the drivers on the nation's roadways who had not been trained by our father.

He had strong feelings about the makes of automobiles, as well as their operation. The only cars I ever heard him praise unconditionally were the Model T Ford of his youth and the Volkswagen Beetle of mine. To watch him maneuver his six-foot-two-inch frame, like one of his own folding rulers, into the driver's seat of a VW Bug was to witness an engineering miracle in itself, I thought. But he claimed that this was nonsense, and that there was ample room in any Volkswagen for anything a reasonable person might care to put in it. He found these cars so comfortable that on long trips, he told us, he would sometimes sleep in his VW, removing the back of the passenger seat and arranging it so that he could stretch himself out full length on that side of the car, with his feet under the dashboard and his head near the rear window.

"And for a pillow," he told me, "I use my shoe. See?" He then showed me how he could undo the laces and spread the leather flaps wide, thus enabling him to cushion his head where his heel would be, under normal circumstances.

"Yes, I see, of course. What a good idea," I agreed, though I didn't believe a word of it. I thought he was baiting me, as he sometimes did, trying to see how outrageous he could be and still get away with it. But who knows? Sleeping in his shoe? Thinking back, I wouldn't put it past him. He did have huge feet (size 12 or 13), and his footgear was chosen for comfort and quality, rather than style. Most of all, though, I find there is something irresistible about the image of my father's little

car, pulled off the Interstate at some quiet rest area and tucked
in along with the great trailers and trucks and semis that cross
the country every day, with my father himself stretched out
and slumbering full-length down the innards of a Volkswagen,
his head nestled in his insole.

Volkswagen and Ford were at the top of the list, but there
was occasionally another vehicle he admired, at least for a
while. Many years after his family was grown, driving through
the game parks in East Africa in the mid-1960s, my father
came to appreciate the all-around ruggedness of the British-
made Land Rover, and chose these vehicles for his travels in
that part of the world. However, by the time his family traveled
with him, during the winter of 1965, he had discovered a fatal
flaw. The mechanism that opened and closed the windows was
a tediously slow-moving circular device that never failed to
infuriate him with its fussy inefficiency. We spent a month with
him that winter, eight of us camping our way through Kenya
and Tanzania, among lions and wildebeests and gazelles and
giraffes, and every time I opened the window, I heard about
punk design.

Sometimes I felt sorry for the punk designers, doomed by
their own limited understanding to second-rate productivity
all their lives: the people who designed the windows of the
Land Rover, the cylindrical flashlight people, the people who
thought round tables were best supported by four legs, rather
than three. This misconception inevitably made the tables wob-
ble, my father said, illustrating his point with a small round
table that my mother had bought for her new kitchen, in the
smaller house they built in Darien after we had all grown up
and the big house had been sold to another family. Underneath
the offending table there was an odd-looking rectangular ped-
estal, itself dependent upon four legs. One of these perpetually
required wedging with a fold of paper, or shimming with a

piece of wood, to keep the table steady. It was absurd, my father said. A round table practically cried out for three legs, and yet someone had gone to all kinds of trouble to give this one four.

What was obviously needed, he continued with severity, was a tripod. My father said that a tripod, like water, by its very nature would seek its own level, and in so doing ensured steadiness and stability. You could count on a tripod. It made sense.

Sense, stability, steadiness, practicality, and economy, these were words we heard often. Nonetheless, my father did indulge in a few extravagances later in his life. While he continued to maintain that luxury was unnecessary, he also said that expense could sometimes be justified by quality. When he discovered Switzerland, in the 1950s and 1960s, working as a consultant for Pan American Airways in Europe, one or two exquisite folding Swiss alarm clocks found their way into our lives, along with several pair of slim and elegant binoculars for my mother's bird-watching. There was also a sausagelike series of fat black Mont Blanc pens, which we filled elaborately, if sluggishly, from inkwells. My father, when he gave me one of these pens, carefully showed me how to fill it, demonstrating a system that I encountered again at Tupperware parties in New England, where it was called, by the salesperson there, "burping" your Tupperware container. My father taught us how to burp the Mont Blanc pens, letting the ink come in while forcing the air out, to avoid accidents.

Accidents were very important to avoid, in my father's house, because the ink was permanent, and my father was deeply and variously sensitive to the concept of permanence. He bought only brass paper clips, because they would not rust on one's important documents, and he used only permanent ink, in the creation of these documents, to ensure their readability for generations to come. Conversely, he believed that certain kinds of human self-indulgence, including obscenity, "tomfoolery," and psychotherapy, generally should be avoided. These too, he felt, were in a sense indelible. Their influences and implications could remain "on your record" forever, sure as the inkstains on your shirt.

I always wondered about "the record" when he talked about it, and I still do. Where is it? Who keeps it? In his presence I secretly scoffed at the whole idea, believing that the only record-keeper I ever really had to worry about was my father himself, with all his systems and all his odd notions. I didn't believe that anyone was counting my paper clips or my therapy sessions. How absurd! I have to confess, though, that he did plant seeds of doubt in my mind. To this day, when I seem to use up cheap steel paper clips by the dozens, and to lose ballpoint pens by the hundreds, in the back of my mind there is the fear that those acts of carelessness, along with all the other blots on my reputation and character, are accumulating silently, dripping like permanent, ink-dark acid on my record, wherever it may now reside. My only hope is that the record-keepers of my own generation are less meticulous than those of my father's, and more like me. They have long since forgotten how to burp a fountain pen, and they can no longer remember where they put the permanent ink.

4
Checklists

✳ OUR father traveled a good deal of the time, as a consultant for Pan American Airways or for the U.S. government, and during my later childhood in connection with his own conservation work. When my father was away, my mother took care of us, assisted by someone hired to help in the running of our household—a secretary or a "nurse."

Most of the nurses are a vague memory for me, as they were present only during my earliest childhood. They would be called "Nannies" now, that series of single women, most often middle-aged or older, who stayed in our house and cared for us when we were very young. Jon and Land speak with affection of "Soeur Lisi," a Swiss woman who was part of the household when they were growing up, while Anne and Scott used to talk about someone whose face I don't remember at all, but whose name as I understood it had been "Miss Galore" (actually Miss Glore). This nurse, I was told, had been a forbidding, Draconian figure whose harsh rules and dietary strictures plagued my siblings' preschool years. I had a later and much happier memory of a warm-hearted, brown-haired local woman, Elsie Knobel, whose nieces went to my school and whose family owned Knobel Brothers' Hardware Store, to my mind the most interesting place of business in town.

Later on there were secretaries who lived with us, after we were too old for the nurses. The secretaries too came for short periods, two or three years at a time, and tended to be younger than the nurses. Their duties consisted of typing my parents' manuscripts, handling bills and correspondence, and doing some amount of driving and shopping and child care, as needed. They lived, one at a time, in the little guest room across the hall from my sister's bedroom, wore perfume and make-up, and owned elaborate, fascinating underwear that sometimes hung on a hook over the towel rack in the bathroom.

The other long-term member of our household was Martha Knecht, a widow from Bavaria, who came to cook for the family when I was in elementary school and lived in our home until our family went to Switzerland, in 1960. Martha's two specialties were Wiener Schnitzel and molasses cookies, which she baked several times a week and kept for us in a round cookie tin in one corner of the dining room.

When my father came home from one of his trips, he wore his navy pinstripe suit and his gray fedora, and he carried the fat calfskin briefcase that also served him as a suitcase. When he walked through the front door, everyone in the family knew it was time to settle down, to shape up, and to pay attention—especially to him.

If we children knew in advance which day he was going to return, which was not always the case, we would spend the days beforehand in two ways. First we would try to *find* things, those things that would inspire his wrath if he found them himself, like the garden rake left out in the rain under the maple tree, with unraked wet leaves all around it, or the salty wet bath towels that still hung, smelly and despondent, on the hooks behind our bathroom doors (we were supposed to use beach towels, not bath towels, for swimming in the cove, and we were supposed to hang them outside to dry), or the lids of the trash cans that had been used as shields in swordplay, one afternoon, and still lay scattered on the floor of the garage, near the garden stakes that had been used as swords.

Next we would try to *remember* things, those things that we knew our father would ask us about as soon as he had, first of all, unpacked his briefcase, and secondly, looked at his lists.

Unpacking would not take him long. He traveled with more papers than clothing anyway, and he carried the briefcase with him on the airplane. It was his practice never to check any luggage. He took no more than a very few items of actual apparel on his trips, no matter how far away he was going or how long he was planning to be away. He packed exactly two of everything: trousers, socks, underwear, and two drip-dry nylon shirts which he had bought for traveling. He washed these out himself, in his hotel bathroom, then hung them up to dry in his window on two folding, inflatable, electric blue traveling coat hangers he carried with him, which looked, when he blew them up to demonstrate, like a pair of water wings. I still imagine my father's view of each faraway city, Paris or Monrovia or Rome or Constantinople, as an obscured and intermittent vision whose strangeness was made familiar to him literally through his own laundry, that lens of pale blue drip-dry nylon swinging in the foreign wind.

The unpacking was simple, but the lists were another story. Some people believe that the most important thing Charles Lindbergh contributed to the field of aviation was not the flight in the *Spirit of St. Louis,* but the safety checklist. I have mixed feelings about this theory, though I think it may be correct. As a pilot my father habitually kept comprehensive lists on all his equipment and all his flying procedures. He checked and rechecked these constantly to make sure that everything he did before, during, and after each flight was appropriate, and that

the aircraft was kept in top condition. It was a habit that saved
his life more than once, and it most likely saved the lives of
many other fliers who followed him. Yet those who lived with
him found that our lives, like the airplanes, were also moni-
tored by checklists (one per child), and for us there was about
his list making, and checking, and rechecking, an invitation to
anxiety, a degree of tedium, and a certain measure of gloom.

I knew, for instance, that when my father returned to Connecticut he would call me into his office within twenty-four
hours, then look at the current list to see what was written
under my name. All of our names were there, each underlined
at the head of its own column, in his neatly slanted, penciled
print: *Jon, Land, Anne, Scott, Reeve*. Some of the columns were
long, others were short. One or two items in each column had
a check mark penciled to the left of it, or a line drawn through
the word entirely. Most, however, did not. That was why we
were summoned into his office. There was much to be thought
about, when our father came home, and even more to be done.

I did not think it was honorable to try to read a sibling's list,
but by the time my father had scanned mine, I already knew
what was on it. I had learned to read his lists upside down
almost as soon as I could read at all. From where I was standing
in the doorway, at the very beginning of my visit to his office,
I could usually estimate how long it would be before I could
leave again. Were there many items in the column under my
name, or just a few? And were they specific, tangible concerns,
like "rake left out in rain," for which I could apologize and
then leave the office, or were they of a more general nature,
like "reading comics" or "chewing gum," which would require
discussion, and take more time? And woe betide me if there
was something really big written on my list, like "Freedom and
Responsibility." Freedom and Responsibility were good for half
an hour, sometimes half an hour each.

There was a "Freedom and Responsibility" lecture—"If you're going to have freedom, you must have responsibility"— applied to anything from dating boys to coming to the dinner table on time. There was an "Instinct and Intellect" lecture, about appreciating nature, using common sense, and not get- ting carried away with contemporary trends, "fuzzy" ideas, or fancy advertising gimmicks. That one sometimes included a discussion of the unnecessary expense of modern toys, and ended with, "Why, when I was your age, I was perfectly happy to play all day with just a stick and a piece of string!"

There was also a "Downfall of Civilization" lecture, prompted by our father's encounters with air conditioning, television, politics, Pop Art, or Mother's Day and Father's Day. These he felt were insincere, commercially inspired artificial holidays. He therefore would not allow us to celebrate them at our house. We could not overtly disobey him, but if he was away when Mother's Day came around, we garlanded our mother's place at the table with flowers, showered her with crayoned greeting cards, mine covered with princesses and flowers and hearts, and reveled in our defiant sentimentality.

Sometimes, in his discussions, our father would refer to Arnold Toynbee, Rudyard Kipling, Calvin Coolidge, or Lao-tzu. After a rumination on the nature of government, for instance, he might quote to me from the Tao Te Ching:

> *"Governing a large country*
> *is like frying a small fish.*
> *You spoil it by too much poking."*

And then he would laugh out loud.

"Yes, Father," I always replied, from the doorway.

When he had just come home from a trip, though, he was

most likely to ask me something practical, like this: what was the actual cost, in dollars and cents, plus tax, of the new pair of ice skates I had persuaded my mother to buy for me during his absence? He did not necessarily object to such a purchase, but he insisted that I know how much had been spent, so that I would understand the value of money, and not take my advantages for granted.

We did not have regular "allowances" of money, as many of our friends did. If we wanted to buy something that was not strictly necessary, something we just wanted, like a doll or a pet mouse, we had to earn the price of it by raking the gravel driveway, or cutting the grass, or doing other jobs around the property. Once in a while I got paid for a feat of stamina or bravery, though. My father gave me a five-dollar bribe for inner-tubing with him and the older children through some fast water in Maine, and another time promised me a penny per second to stand on my head. When I stayed up for an unexpected five minutes and twenty seconds, he paid up, every penny. He always kept his promises.

There were some items, like the ice skates, that were by some miracle considered "necessary," especially by our mother. But if I could not tell my father what they cost the first day he asked, he would call me into his office again the next day, and I would see my name on the checklist again. By reading upside down, again, I would see that at the top of the list under my name was still the word "Skates." It would be there every day, and so would I, until he got the answer he was waiting for.

At first, when he came back from being away, I felt nothing but unbridled joy at my father's return. I would leap down the stairs when I heard the big door open, and I would throw myself into his arms. It was a thrill to feel the tall shape of him again, and to breathe in the deep sober scents of travel and gray hat and dark suit, mingling with the more homelike paternal odors of leather and pencil shavings and clean-clipped fingernails and the great Connecticut outdoors.

He would give me a short, strong hug in return, accompanied by a happy grunt—"Whuoof!"—as if my enthusiasm had knocked the air out of him. I would look up then to see him laughing, with the wide grin that wrinkled the skin around his eyes, and I would feel surprise that his eyes were lighter blue than I remembered, more like the Caribbean than the Atlantic, and not like my mother's, which were the color of blueberries along the coast of Maine.

Instead of asking me whether I had been good or bad during his absence, my father would feel my forehead with his fingers for "nubbins," his word for the beginnings of devil's horns, and then reach around to my shoulder blades to see if I was growing any feathers, for angel wings. This made me laugh, because I was ticklish, and then to chatter and giggle and hop up and down and dissolve into generalized silliness.

My father put a stop to this at once.

"Now, now!" he'd say sharply. "Watch out for my hat!"

I was barely tall enough to reach his neck, with my outflung arms. I could not possibly harm his hat. But I would stop, crestfallen, and then I would remember what my father was really like. He loved his children, and he was equal to any real crisis, but he hated chatter and he hated chaos. He exercised affection and discipline in equal measure, often at the same time. When our young German shepherd, Siggy, rushed to greet him, the dog would be wriggling with uncontrollable adoration toward my father's outstretched hand, working himself into a state, writhing and rolling on the floor when the homecoming fingers caressed his head. But Siggy would draw back as if at an electric shock at the stern, deep-voiced, "Enough!"

Like Siggy, I would subside immediately at the change in tone, feeling at once embraced and chastised. In a confusion of devotion and resentment, I became a passive witness to other greetings. My mother and sister both hugged my father, as I had done. (If they got the warning about the hat, I didn't hear it.) My brothers, because they were men, shuffled their feet and shrugged their shoulders and grinned and shook his hand.

We all stayed right there, gathered around him, galvanized, revitalized, and entirely self-conscious. When our father came through the front door after an absence it was as if the family suddenly woke up again, each of us into a vivid and conflicting set of emotions. Suddenly we felt all of our feelings much more acutely: happiness, excitement, nervousness, and dread. As soon as our father entered the house we snapped, as if out of hypnosis, into a more than military alertness. In his presence we became much more completely, and more perilously, alive.

It was about then that I would find myself beginning to wonder, though, right in the midst of all the greetings and all the excitement, before my father had even fully entered the house, just how long it would be before he put on his navy pinstripe suit and his gray fedora, packed his briefcase, walked out through the front door again, and left us in peace. And I would grumble silently to myself, as we all walked with the returning head of our household through the dark entryway and into the larger, lighter spaces of hall and stairwell and living room, "I wasn't anywhere *near* his hat."

My father's hat, like his "manuscript"—whatever piece of writing he was working on, whether it be *The Spirit of St. Louis* or a letter to the Minnesota Historical Society—was not to be trifled with. When he was not traveling, he kept the hat on a high shelf in his narrow bedroom closet, which had a lower shelf for shoes at the level of my knees, and smelled pungently of cedar. The hat had its own spot, too high for me to reach, near a pile of white handkerchiefs and just behind a wooden box with a sliding cover, containing the loose change he stored there when he hung his pants in the closet. My sister and I had each pilfered this box more than once, when the hat and its owner were both far away, and when our mother was temporarily out of the house. We would step on the low shelf, our bare feet parting the polished pairs of black and brown shoes lined up side by side, our thieving fingers groping for the change box, our hearts beating too hard and too close to our ribs.

I don't know why we stole his money. It wasn't worth the risk. Neither of us ever dared to take more than two or three coins at a time, a couple of nickels and a dime, or some pennies and one quarter, never two. And I at least was so terrified during the whole time I was engaged in the theft that I was in real danger of wetting my pants, leaving behind me terrible evidence of my sins right on top of my father's shoes.

I could feel during these episodes a rising nausea, a ringing in my ears, and a pounding in my chest, symptoms of the belief that my father, no matter where he was in the world at that specific moment, would instantly be aware of my thievery. Even as my greedy fingers slid open the box and groped for the coins, he would know what I was up to. He would suddenly stand still, in Lausanne, or Munich, or Anchorage, or Monrovia. He would tilt his head down to hear the whispers of his own omniscient inner voice, and he would be on to me. Immediately he would vanish, genielike, from whatever place had kept him busy on the other side of the earth, just disappear in a flash of light or in a cloud of acrid orange smoke the way the Wicked Witch of the West had done. Immediately he would materialize again right here in his own bedroom, his light blue eyes cold and yet at the same time unimaginably searing, like dry ice. He would stand before me in the full and towering knowledge that his own private and personal closet door had been opened, and his own personal and private loose change box had been invaded. And at that instant—what else could he do?—my father would strike me dead.

5
A Nonbenevolent Dictatorship

⁂ W H E N my father left home on his travels, the first emptiness I felt was verbal. There was so much less talk when he was gone: no more warnings, admonitions, or instructions, no lectures on preparedness for the "unforeseen," no philosophizings about the universe, theorizings about the government, or predictions concerning the downfall of Western Civilization. There were no more sudden blistering chastisements, or those double-edged "discussions" I hated, in which one of his children was first asked to give an opinion on something, and then criticized for the way the opinion was delivered, something I felt was extremely unjust.

In family arguments, it seemed to me that my father didn't fight fair, a real sin according to my childhood ethic. Arguing with him could be frustrating to the point of incoherent fury. Once when I was in my teens, for instance, he and I were discussing Andy Warhol's Campbell's Soup can paintings. I had seen them, at the MOMA, and I liked them. My father hated them, sight unseen, as soon as he heard from me that such paintings even existed. He immediately consigned Warhol and all his works to the Downfall of Civilization list. When I protested, trying to conduct the argument on its merits (Did Warhol's Campbell's Soup cans count as art, or not?), my father broke off the whole discussion to question my taste, malign my friends (with whom was I associating, that I had developed such strange opinions?), and then criticize my speech itself: I talked too fast, he said, "like a Gatling gun," and I did not pronounce my words carefully.

While I was still sputtering, he changed his tone completely, smiled fondly at me, and said, "You really must learn to enunciate, Reevekins."

I was thrown off guard, if not entirely disarmed, by his calling me a pet name at such a moment. (I was the youngest child, and somewhat spoiled, as my sister had often pointed out to me.) But he was mistaken if he thought that he could use these wiles to take the sting out of his criticism.

He had made me so angry that I wanted to tell him that my enunciation no doubt bothered him because he was hard of hearing, but I didn't dare. He never admitted this, and I would never have dared to suggest it. Not only that, but I also knew that he was right, I did talk too fast. We all have our faults and failings, and I consoled myself by thinking that if he pointed out mine while I refrained from pointing out his, then maybe I was a better person.

However, I was bold enough to offer my opinion that it was undemocratic that *he* could say whatever he wanted to, in an argument, but that what *I* said was subject to review, not only for content but for style.

"This is not a democracy," he replied, grinning at me with a mixture of mockery and affection. "This is a nonbenevolent dictatorship." It was a favorite saying of his, and he laughed after he said it, but I didn't. I wasn't in the mood.

We were all called to account regularly for our opinions and our plans and our current behavior, and our father would freely characterize these as he saw fit, at any time. Perhaps he sought to understand his five children through some form of conceptual containment, perhaps to hold us a little longer as we grew up and away from his influence. What he actually said about us didn't matter so much, I think, and it changed, anyway, over the years. It was the saying, the repetition and the manner of it, that made us his, forever.

I always felt, though, that my father's opinions built a box around me that was much too small for my personality, and I frankly hated hearing his thoughts about my brothers and sisters, except for Jon, who was grown and gone by the time I was old enough to listen to my father. He generally spoke of Jon as an adult, someone who under his tutelage had turned out well. But I remember him referring to Land as "a cowboy" in an uncomplimentary way, whenever he felt that Land's spirits were too high or his activities unruly; and I remember also that he warned me, as if to discourage any idea I might have of emulating my sister, that Anne could be "too clever for her own good" (*Too smart, too funny, too quick for you, Father?* I thought, pleased at the notion, proud of Anne's humor, her defiant independence). He continued to criticize my quick speech and my impetuous opinions well into my college years and beyond, shaking his head over "those Radcliffe ideas" (passionate opposition to the Vietnam War, anger at race and gender injustice) that I brought back from my undergraduate days in Cambridge.

Mysteriously, he was hardest of all on Scott, who never seemed to me to deserve his anger at all, let alone so much of it. Scott could get along with most people, and with all animals. He almost convinced me that the friendliest pet a person could ever hope to have was a hog-nosed snake, and once created a boric acid salve, on his own, in order to help me clean the eye of a pet turtle no bigger than a silver dollar. If I was afraid of the dark and told him so, Scott would come and sleep in my room, without telling anybody else in the family his reason for being there. When my father instructed me, at an early age, to "dump this garbage behind the kitchen door," and then spanked me later when he found that I had done exactly that, not understanding that he meant "in the garbage can," Scott went out and cleaned up the mess while I was still sobbing in my room.

Scott has always been both gentle-hearted and absent-minded, and when he was growing up he tended to lose things and forget things even more than the rest of us did. When he was old enough to drive both a car and a motorboat, Scott went out into the middle of Long Island Sound one summer day with all the family car keys in his pocket. My father, characteristically, had made duplicates, but somehow Scott had those with him, too. The family was completely without transportation until he returned several hours later. Our father's wrath was terrible to behold, and worse to hear, when he scolded Scott afterward.

"Scott! I have told you over and over and OVER again," our father would begin, in these scoldings, his voice growing louder and louder as he gained momentum. He told Scott that he was irresponsible, that he never listened, that he was behaving like "an adolescent ass." He told Scott that he, our father, was "disgusted and disappointed," and on and on, while Scott bent his head a little, but stood his ground until our father had finished. And when it was over, the air still ringing with the sound and force of the words that had just been said, Scott would look up at our father, his face flushed but his eyes dry, and he would speak quietly.

"Yes, Father. I'm sorry, Father." And then Scott would walk away with his shoulders hunched forward and his eyes on the ground, back to his animals.

When he grew up, Scott went to live in England, and then in France, and finally moved to Brazil, where he lives now, working with endangered species. For some years in the late 1960s, he and our father did not see each other at all, though they sent each other long letters across the oceans and continents that now separated them. Finally, when our father was dying in 1974, Scott flew home to visit him in the hospital in New York, and they spent hours together, talking. I don't know what was said, on either side, but when Anne and I called our father at this same time, telephoning from Maine, where we were staying together with our young children, he spoke to me of Scott's "wisdom" and "vision" and "depth." He told me that Scott was like our grandfather Morrow, a comparison that made me smile. Dwight Morrow, ambassador to Mexico, was a man of unusual diplomatic skill, and legendary absentmindedness.

When my father was away, the energy vacuum was even greater than the verbal one. I might not miss his lectures, but I missed his bounding up the stairs, skipping several of them on his way, and humming the shapeless, toneless tune that Anne, behind his back, called "The Minnesota Funeral Dirge." When he was absent there were no more family walks, no gatherings together in front of the living room fire while he read Rudyard Kipling's *The Jungle Book,* no evenings out on the porch watching the weather, no sunsets and no storms. His physical absence also left us with an absence of physical parental affection, as he was always by far the more physically affectionate of our parents, though he would not allow this side of himself to show in public. By habit and self-discipline, as long as I knew him, he tried to hide even the happiest moments of his family life from curious eyes. It was as if the very act of admitting family happiness, exposing it to public view, would somehow destroy it, as it had been destroyed once before.

All the same, there were back-rubs and bear-hugs, long rides on his shoulders during the daytime and bedtime games after we were tucked in at night. He would parade a collection of imaginary animals across our backs, naming each one: "Sammy the Turtle" lumbered between my shoulder blades every night, represented by my father's big callused fingers; "Socky the Skunk" had a rocking-chair gait created by the combined movements of his knuckled fist and soft palm, and sometimes he made me laugh to the point of near hysteria with a ticklish scamper of squirrels up and down my spine, introducing them as "Mr. Little, Mrs. Little, and ALL the little-little Littles." (My mother would have to come in and settle me down again, with a half-amused, half-disapproving, "Oh, Charles!")

Our mother's love for her children was no less deep, but her expressions of love were gentle, often verbal, and just as often unspoken and yet completely understood by every one of her children. Where our father's words could scourge and sting, her words, her mere presence in a house, would heal, soothe, and uplift us. Even now, walking into a room where she sits, not ever sure at any meeting between us that she will know where she is or who I am, I become calmer and surer as I walk closer to her, step by step. I am so instinctively confident of her love that it sustains me even when it does not, perhaps, sustain her.

But she has an innate, immediately perceivable bodily reserve. One kisses her lightly, hugs her softly, with the understanding that it is imperative to leave the intimacy of her physical space, and of her body, inviolate. This has always been true, as was our father's surprising, instinctive physical affection and playfulness during private moments with his family.

When our father left us to travel around the world, and even when he left the world entirely, at his death in 1974, there was an element of relief in his absence, some quietness that we had not ever known in our lives before. But he left behind a vast hole in our universe, as great as the death of a star.

6
She Must Be Lonely

✳ WHEN our mother walked out through the front door of the old house in Connecticut, it was usually for a day in the city. She would be carrying a black velvet handbag, and wearing her stockings as well as her city coat and hat and shoes. I had secret knowledge, as I watched her through the window, that she was also wearing a lace-edged garter belt around her waist, and that it held up her stockings by means of a system of buttons and hooks that must be tickling her upper legs even as she walked down the path to the car.

My mother had explained garter belts to me, along with brassieres, one day when I was visiting her in her bathroom. She liked to soak in a tub of deep, hot water with soap bubbles in it, drizzling her shoulders periodically with more hot water, soaking up the water and the bubbles with a big shapeless sponge that was the color of light brown sugar and had holes all through it, and looked to me like a human brain. When the sponge was so full of water that it had turned dark brown, she would let it drip in a luxurious way over her shoulders and down her back, and she would close her eyes and smile.

I could never tell whether my mother's dark hair was long or short when I was a child. It was curly in front and pulled back at the sides, often tied with a colored ribbon, and in the bath it was bound up tight around her head in a sash that seemed to be made of string, like a fishnet. Her lingerie hung all around her over her head, on a series of hangers and clotheslines that spiderwebbed the ceiling above my parents' bathtub. The straps and hooks and lace arrangements, the steel hangers and the pieces of clothesline, the scented, bubbly water and the sponge, together dangled before my eyes ambiguous visions of quietness and contentment, of sophistication and hidden entanglements, my mother at home and in New York City.

I knew that when she was dressed up and had a handbag, she was heading for the very heart of New York, where her sister-in-law, our Aunt Margot, had an apartment on East 77th Street. (Margot had been married to my mother's brother, Dwight, and remained close to the family.) There she would attend a monthly meeting, with several other similarly dressed women, whom she collectively called "My Group." They would sit together in my aunt's apartment, and meditate, looking nowhere and saying nothing for a long time, and then they would discuss authors and titles whose names I could read silently off the spines of the books piled on the table near my mother's bed, but would not have dared to attempt pronouncing out loud: *The Divine Milieu,* by Teilhard de Chardin, *Winter's Tales* by Isak Dinesen, *Think on These Things* by Krishnamurti. I once caught a glimpse of *Cheri* and *The Last of Cheri,* both by the French writer Colette, and asked about them, but my mother quickly hid those behind the others, and blushed. I don't think they were on the reading list.

I knew, on Group days, that my mother was going to walk through the front door and out of my life for the day as soon as she began to powder her nose and put on her lipstick. The powder came from a square gold compact with a little piece of broken mirror inside, and a powder-drenched tuft of cotton

instead of a powder puff. A French verse was printed on the
outside in raised letters:

> *Il pleure dans mon coeur*
> *Comme il pleut sur la ville;*
> *Quelle est cette langueur*
> *Qui pénètre mon coeur?*

I learned when my mother translated it for me that this was
a sad verse about heartbreak and rain, and later in my life,
when I was living in Paris as a student among wet sidewalks
and gray pigeons, I remembered it. The poem, by Paul Ver-
laine, has always made me think about the women everywhere
around the world, with their gold compacts and their tiny
broken mirrors, who have powdered their noses in complicated bathrooms, and covered up their tears.

Her lipstick was red, never pink, and she applied it in a
mysterious manner. There were several gold Helena Rubinstein
lipstick tubes in her bathroom, and in each of these tubes,
when I inspected them, the lipstick had not been flattened and
mushed down into its cylinder with use, the way I flattened
and mushed mine later on. Instead it had been worn into a
bright, deep concavity, with two high points forming a groove
between which she ran her lips. I tried and tried to copy her
technique, but I never could put on lipstick the way my mother
did. It was another sign of her uniqueness among women, I
thought, that quiet difference that gave me a sense of meaning
and peace in the midst of all mysteries. And on the days when
I saw my mother walk away down the path to the driveway,
leaving our family to step into the car that would take her to
the city, I felt the gray house losing warmth, felt it withdraw
entirely into itself, and absorb the chill and dampness into
every stone.

The house was not made entirely of stone, but there was a stone foundation, and stonework on the first floor. Stones had been used to create three ground-floor porches overlooking Scott's Cove, the little inlet of Long Island Sound alongside which the house was built. One of these porches, just under my own bedroom, was screened on three sides, while the fourth opened into the dining room through a glass door in a wall that was completely covered on the inside by curtains. They hung from ceiling to floor, and were decorated with a blue-and-white French provincial pattern that my mother must have chosen. They looked like something that would have been in one of her own mother's homes, with implications of foreign languages and good manners, and a touch of teasing frivolity. From where I sat at the dining room table, I could follow shepherds and maidens coyly pursuing one another all the way up and down the curtains, and in and out of their multiple folds across the wall, but I don't remember seeing any sheep.

The square screened porch beyond the curtains, like the dark entryway on the other side of the house by the arched front door, was cool even in the salted mugginess of August in Darien because of its deep and stony shade. We sometimes ate our evening meals out there, around a glass-topped table, and then we could watch the darkness come in over the cove down below us, over the little rocky islands and the pine trees on the point. As it got darker, we would hear the pulsing buzz of katydids beginning to fill the air, first just a little bit and then more and more, until there was no other noise in the night, and the night was everywhere around us.

I once sat with my mother for an hour there on a summer evening, waiting to see a moonflower bloom. The plant itself was set in a large ceramic pot on the table, and the flower when it eventually opened was white and headily fragrant, like a camellia. It uncurled in a slow spiral at its appointed time, not smoothly as in time-lapse photography, but with little jerks of motion that were more convincing to me than smoothness, even then. Nature's openings, and her closings, too, are not so easy, in my experience, and are usually anything but smooth. They are hesitant and awkward, and frequently unwilling, even if inevitable. I want to hold my breath at birth and death, each time I come close to them. I want to close my eyes and pray, without certainty of any kind, that everyone involved will somehow make it through.

Beyond my mother's screened moonflower porch was the broad, tiled, family porch, stretching across the front of the house. It was open to the cove, and it backed up against the living room window, so that the wide stretch of glass reflected the whole of the cove and sky. If you sat outside to watch the sun go down, the view was the same in both directions. The furniture here seemed massive: a wooden settee, as my father called it, with a rope frame that held a bulky blue cushion the size of a mattress for a double bed, and wooden chairs with thick, brown, sloping slats and big pairs of wheels by which they could be moved in a laborious and squeaky way into different positions on the tiles. Some of the furniture was flimsier, with light canvas and bright cushions, and one chaise longue seemed to be made entirely of thin white rope, the kind used for sailboats, wound a million times, spool-like, around a black metal frame.

This was the place my father liked to sit in the evenings when he was home, in the middle of the settee with his wife and children around him, reaching out his arms across the canvas cushions, drawing us close together to watch the play of sun and water and sky and storm cloud, under his wing. This porch was the place where my brother Land played Hank Snow songs on his guitar late at night, humming and singing and strumming alone under my window long after I had been sent to bed. He may not have known anyone was listening, but I went to sleep many nights to the music of lonesome prairies, lost romances, and powerful locomotives, rocked and lulled by the *Golden River,* or riding into the rhythms of my dreams on *The Wabash Cannonball.*

I had my hair cut short there every summer before I went to camp, tears streaming down my face each time, whether because of anticipated homesickness during the eight weeks away, or for fear of the scissors in my mother's hand. She never made a mistake, she just snipped carefully and sighed while I cried, and she said several times that it wouldn't be long now, and then finally the snipping stopped, and she brushed the short hairs off my neck with a towel, and swept the long ones up with a broom and dustpan, for the birds.

"They eat them?" I asked my mother, astonished.

"They use them for building their nests," she said.

This idea, for some reason, cheered me up completely.

Once, when my father was away, I saw Corliss Lamont on the family porch, and thought he did not belong there. He was one of my mother's closest friends since earliest childhood, and one of her "beaux" in college. That day he was striding back and forth as if on a vaudeville stage, waving his arms and wearing a striped shirt and bright red trousers. He smiled and gesticulated at my mother while she watched him, straight-backed, and upright, rather than in her usual reclining position, on the ropy chaise longue. Her back was to me, so I could not tell what she thought of the performance.

Corliss Lamont had bushy eyebrows that seemed to stay up high on his forehead in perpetual happy surprise, and a thick-textured voice with a sort of growl in it. He wore what I thought of as extremely stylish clothes, the kind that my father would not have been caught dead in: plaids and tweeds and

bright-colored cottons, and although I think even Corliss Lamont drew the line at madras Bermuda shorts, I'm not prepared to swear to it. Like my mother, he was the child of an
early J.P. Morgan partner, Thomas Lamont, and he was raised
in affluence, as she was. But he became a teacher and a philoso-
pher, a humanist and a champion of humanitarian causes, and
he once successfully defied the federal government and the
U.S. Post Office during a legal battle over the censorship of his
mail.

Corliss Lamont loved to ski, to dance, and to sing. In his
later life he recorded poems and love songs, in that same
benign, aristocratic growl. There is no doubt in my mind whatsoever that Corliss knew who Elvis Presley was. He probably
could even dance the lindy.

I was inside that day, watching my mother and Mr. Lamont
through the living room window, and I could not hear what
either of them was saying. When I told my sister about the
scene, many years later, she just shrugged.

"He was probably proposing to her again," she said.

I was shocked. Mr. Lamont was, usually, just as married as
our mother was—in fact he was much more married, three
times, at least two of them very happy marriages, by my mother's own estimate. But Anne still claimed that Corliss Lamont
had only gotten married in the first place, and again in the
second and third, because he had not been able to persuade
our mother to accept him. Between wives, Anne theorized, he
just kept on trying. Anne told me that our mother, as a widow
in the 1970s, had said to her one day in an abstracted, thoughtful way, "You know, I think the next time Corliss proposes to
me, I really should say no." Anne longed to ask our mother
what she had said all the other times, but she never did.

We had guests at the house quite frequently when my parents were both home, but the guests came from far away, not

neighboring houses or towns. My parents did not seem to have any local friends at all. Couples drove out from New York for the evening for dinner, or stayed at the house for a night or two when they were passing through our part of the country. Our aunts and uncles visited with their families, as did people my parents knew through their aviation and publishing careers, and old friends they had known during the years when they lived abroad.

When my father was away, though, my mother's friends would come to keep her company, one by one. They would sit with her in the living room having tea, or outside on the family porch watching the egrets in the cove at low tide. These were artists, writers, dancers, sometimes psychologists or teachers, but not so often businesspeople or aviators. My mother's friends would talk to her about literature and religion and art and insight. They would bring her books, and music, and sometimes plants, like the moonflower.

The men, too, like Corliss Lamont, came to see her individually. They visited when my father was home, of course, but they often came again when he was away, without their wives, if they had any. The men also came for tea, and they also sat and talked thoughtfully with my mother during the long afternoons, one by one. There was Dr. Dana Atchley of Columbia Presbyterian Medical Center, whose thinning hair stuck up from his head in a little white tuft, and who told stories about Adlai Stevenson. There was Jack Huber, psychologist, writer, and teacher, and an old friend of Aunt Margot's, and there was David Read, a young psychiatrist who had come to the house first as a friend of Judy Guild, one of my parents' youngest and liveliest secretaries, but stayed on as a family friend. All of these men visited in a respectable and proper manner, but all of them, I knew, felt sorry for her because her husband was so often away. They thought she must be lonely without him, and

I am sure they were right, much of the time. But regardless of her visitors, male or female, I think that some of the time, when he was away, she was just as relieved as we were.

I don't know at what age I learned that my mother was a writer, beloved by millions of readers around the world. I think I was very young, certainly too young to read or write myself. It wasn't until many years later that I became reconciled to her profession, and it was later still when, to my surprise, I made this same profession my own. In the beginning, though, her literary work was only an inexplicable interruption in the mother-child relationship—a sad cross for a sensitive child to bear.

What I disliked most about her writing was that it separated her from me physically, by means of a closed door. When she was in her "writing room" in the house in Connecticut, we children were forbidden by our father to disturb her. I often did this anyway, if I thought I could get away with it, usually at a time when my father was outside chopping wood, or was himself engrossed in his own writing project in his own office, downstairs. Nobody would think of disturbing *him* when the door was closed and he was tapping away with two fingers on his old Royal typewriter, working on *The Spirit of St. Louis*.

I had no interest in my father's flying or his writing career, but I thought that surely my mother did not *really* want to be shut away for a whole afternoon with a pen and a pad of paper, without seeing my face, hearing my thoughts, inspecting my bruises, or in some other way affirming for both of us the extraordinary importance of my presence in her life.

I knew this was true because if I knocked on my mother's door, she always answered, and if I entered the room, she never seemed to mind. She would put down her pen immediately, and smile gently, and ask what I wanted. (See? She *was* con-

Sound, mallard ducks swimming in and out of the marsh grasses of the saltwater bays and inlets of Scott's Cove, and ducks and geese floating on our neighbor's pond. There were also chickadees and sparrows and an occasional bright red cardinal visiting our bird feeder, while pheasants moved with furtive dignity across the back borders of the lawn. My mother scattered cracked corn there every morning after breakfast for all the ground-feeding birds, carrying it out across the yard in a long-necked, white enamel pitcher. In the afternoons, she took a bag of crumbs down to the cove, and cast her bread upon the waters.

There were many kinds of bread to be cast: buttered scraps of English muffin from our breakfast, and Pepperidge Farm crusts from our lunchtime peanut-butter-and-strawberry-jam sandwiches. There was no Wonder Bread, Marshmallow Fluff, or even grape jelly for our family. My father's maternal grandfather, Charles Land, had been a dentist in Detroit, and my father never forgot his teachings. We ate no candy—or at least we ate no candy that our father knew about; we brushed our teeth vigorously every night and morning with Ammodent tooth powder in the blue-and-white can, and as for those peanut butter sandwiches, we considered ourselves lucky to get the jam.

Sometimes, if our mother took her walk late in the day, the waterfowl got raisin toast, crumbled from her five o'clock tea. The ducks came gliding toward her in the evening light by twos and threes, while the Canada geese made rippled hovering circles farther out, waiting until she left the scene before they dared to approach the feed. Often a single great blue heron would preside over the whole ritual from a safe and muddy distance, the stillness of its curved neck and stiltlike legs marking an extraordinary elegance, even in the mud at low tide.

cerned about my needs, above all else, I thought triumphantly. What did my father know? *Nothing.*) She sat in a straight-backed chair by the window, at a desk that was really just a flat table with a blotter on it, and little more. I could see only a pen tray, holding one or two shells or feathers in it along with the pens and pencils, and an inkwell, and the blue pad she was writing on. How important could these few things be, compared to me?

There was one leafy maple branch outside the bright window just to the left of my mother's desk. ("It is important to have the light come in over the left shoulder," she advised me, later, when I was setting up my own writing room, in my own house.) I could tell by the way she turned toward the doorway where I stood, with the light from the window on her face, that she was very glad to see me. I knew she would be.

My father, however, was an uncannily perceptive man. No matter how far away I had thought he was, he would inevitably show up at my mother's writing room door at just about this time, looking extremely displeased. He would take me away from my mother's pleasant nest, with its wall filled with bookshelves at one end of the little room, and the old soft leather couch I was about to make myself comfortable in, at the other. He would shut the door behind us, and he would lecture me once again about my mother's creative gifts, about her need for privacy in order to exercise such gifts to their fullest extent, and about my obligation to respect this aspect of her life. Each time I heard his lecture I nodded, and apologized, and told him I understood what he was saying and would try to do better in the future.

I didn't mean a word of it. How could I?

What I did not understand, and only much later began to comprehend, is that my mother's work, that product of our separation, is also the way back to her again. She herself created the pathway, a connection between us that is much deeper and more lasting than any I had ever anticipated in childhood. All I had to do to find it was read her books.

As a child, I did not read my parents' books, ever. First of all, there were no pictures in them, except for the old black-and-white photographs from a time before I was born, or (in my mother's *Gift from the Sea*) a few line drawings of seashells. Boring. Also, I was embarrassed and squeamish about the fact that my parents wrote at all, constantly spilling out their adventures and their theories and philosophies and the most intimate secrets of our lives to complete strangers. To this day, people who have read my mother's *Diaries and Letters* will come up to me and tell me the funny things my brother Jon, now a grandfather, said as a little boy at the breakfast table.

The difference, though, is that now I enjoy this experience. Instead of feeling a child's discomfort at sharing my personal life with the world, I eagerly look to the world, in my middle age, to restore to me what was always mine . . . only I didn't know it.

7
A Noticeable Relaxation

✳ B Y contrast to the force and the flavor of his rule our mother's household management during our father's absences from home was so benign, and her touch on the reins of power so feather-light, that when he went off on a trip there was at first a stalled, deflated feeling in our house, as if the air had been let out of all its tires. Very soon, however, this changed to a sense of release, an exhalation of long-held family breath, and a noticeable relaxation in discipline. Within days or even hours of his departure, an easygoing vacation atmosphere began to steal over our home like the blessed air of Indian summer, and we could feel a delicious looseness leaking into our very bones.

Our schedules were the same, but our lives much easier when our father was away. We ate our meals and went to school and to bed and to our dentist appointments or dancing lessons as usual, but we didn't risk a lecture if we forgot to put our bicycles away, and sometimes we were allowed to drink a glass of ginger ale or 7-Up, with ice in it, even if we weren't sick. Our mother wrote her books, and tended her garden, and saw her friends, and drove carpools, and always, every day, she fed the birds.

We had Canada geese flying over our house on Long Island

cerned about my needs, above all else, I thought triumphantly. What did my father know? *Nothing.*) She sat in a straight-backed chair by the window, at a desk that was really just a flat table with a blotter on it, and little more. I could see only a pen tray, holding one or two shells or feathers in it along with the pens and pencils, and an inkwell, and the blue pad she was writing on. How important could these few things be, compared to me?

There was one leafy maple branch outside the bright window just to the left of my mother's desk. ("It is important to have the light come in over the left shoulder," she advised me, later, when I was setting up my own writing room, in my own house.) I could tell by the way she turned toward the doorway where I stood, with the light from the window on her face, that she was very glad to see me. I knew she would be.

My father, however, was an uncannily perceptive man. No matter how far away I had thought he was, he would inevitably show up at my mother's writing room door at just about this time, looking extremely displeased. He would take me away from my mother's pleasant nest, with its wall filled with bookshelves at one end of the little room, and the old soft leather couch I was about to make myself comfortable in, at the other. He would shut the door behind us, and he would lecture me once again about my mother's creative gifts, about her need for privacy in order to exercise such gifts to their fullest extent, and about my obligation to respect this aspect of her life. Each time I heard his lecture I nodded, and apologized, and told him I understood what he was saying and would try to do better in the future.

I didn't mean a word of it. How could I?

What I did not understand, and only much later began to comprehend, is that my mother's work, that product of our separation, is also the way back to her again. She herself created the pathway, a connection between us that is much deeper and more lasting than any I had ever anticipated in childhood. All I had to do to find it was read her books.

As a child, I did not read my parents' books, ever. First of all, there were no pictures in them, except for the old black-and-white photographs from a time before I was born, or (in my mother's *Gift from the Sea*) a few line drawings of seashells. Boring. Also, I was embarrassed and squeamish about the fact that my parents wrote at all, constantly spilling out their adventures and their theories and philosophies and the most intimate secrets of our lives to complete strangers. To this day, people who have read my mother's *Diaries and Letters* will come up to me and tell me the funny things my brother Jon, now a grandfather, said as a little boy at the breakfast table.

The difference, though, is that now I enjoy this experience. Instead of feeling a child's discomfort at sharing my personal life with the world, I eagerly look to the world, in my middle age, to restore to me what was always mine . . . only I didn't know it.

7
A Noticeable
Relaxation

✳ , B Y contrast to the force and the flavor of his rule, our mother's household management during our father's absences from home was so benign, and her touch on the reins of power so feather-light, that when he went off on a trip there was at first a stalled, deflated feeling in our house, as if the air had been let out of all its tires. Very soon, however, this changed to a sense of release, an exhalation of long-held family breath, and a noticeable relaxation in discipline. Within days or even hours of his departure, an easygoing vacation atmosphere began to steal over our home like the blessed air of Indian summer, and we could feel a delicious looseness leaking into our very bones.

Our schedules were the same, but our lives much easier, when our father was away. We ate our meals and went to school and to bed and to our dentist appointments or dancing lessons as usual, but we didn't risk a lecture if we forgot to put our bicycles away, and sometimes we were allowed to drink a glass of ginger ale or 7-Up, with ice in it, even if we weren't sick. Our mother wrote her books, and tended her garden, and saw her friends, and drove carpools, and always, every day, she fed the birds.

We had Canada geese flying over our house on Long Island

Sound, mallard ducks swimming in and out of the marsh grasses of the saltwater bays and inlets of Scott's Cove, and ducks and geese floating on our neighbor's pond. There were also chickadees and sparrows and an occasional bright red cardinal visiting our bird feeder, while pheasants moved with furtive dignity across the back borders of the lawn. My mother scattered cracked corn there every morning after breakfast for all the ground-feeding birds, carrying it out across the yard in a long-necked, white enamel pitcher. In the afternoons, she took a bag of crumbs down to the cove, and cast her bread upon the waters.

There were many kinds of bread to be cast: buttered scraps of English muffin from our breakfast, and Pepperidge Farm crusts from our lunchtime peanut-butter-and-strawberry-jam sandwiches. There was no Wonder Bread, Marshmallow Fluff, or even grape jelly for our family. My father's maternal grandfather, Charles Land, had been a dentist in Detroit, and my father never forgot his teachings. We ate no candy—or at least we ate no candy that our father knew about; we brushed our teeth vigorously every night and morning with Ammodent tooth powder in the blue-and-white can, and as for those peanut butter sandwiches, we considered ourselves lucky to get the jam.

Sometimes, if our mother took her walk late in the day, the waterfowl got raisin toast, crumbled from her five o'clock tea. The ducks came gliding toward her in the evening light by twos and threes, while the Canada geese made rippled hovering circles farther out, waiting until she left the scene before they dared to approach the feed. Often a single great blue heron would preside over the whole ritual from a safe and muddy distance, the stillness of its curved neck and stiltlike legs marking an extraordinary elegance, even in the mud at low tide.

Once in a while my mother would go farther afield, taking us with her, on long walks over the back roads and across a stone bridge, to a place where larger and more exotic congregations of birds gathered: not only ducks and geese, but even a few swans. We were awed and fascinated by the swans; they seemed creatures from another element entirely, serene as floating feathered clouds. Once, though, my sister Anne unwittingly got between a swan and its cygnets, and was confronted by the full fury of a viciously jabbing black beak, and wild, white beating wings. Terrified, she screamed and backed away, but our mother was already there, shouting at the other, feathered mother, and shooing her away from the frightened child. Afterward, when I heard the story in family retellings, it seemed to me that only Anne, of all the children in the family, would have been attacked by a creature as extreme and as magical as a swan, and only our mother would have been equal to the challenge and the choreography of counterattack.

She has noticed and pointed out winged things to me for as long as I have known her: birds, butterflies, Renaissance angels, ladybugs, wing-shaped shells, a white sweep of cirrus cloud outside the window of her writing room, just behind the maple branches whose pattern itself could be traced as easily on the wing of a dragonfly as on a sky. I in turn used to bring her things that seemed winglike, to win her approval: crayon drawings of princesses whose cone-shaped hats trailed rainbow-colored scarves and whose dresses had golden winglets pushing out from their puffed and purple sleeves; maple seedlings twinned and spinning down through the air onto the flagstone walk between our house and the gravel drive, and feathers.

My mother has collected feathers all her life as readily and as absentmindedly, sometimes, as if they were the shells, or smooth stones, or the horse chestnuts which she has also gathered, picking them up along the seawall at Scott's Cove, and from the beaches in Florida or Hawaii. Sometimes she even found them on little Alpine cow paths that she followed on walks up the mountain just above the place where she spent thirty summers, the first ten of them with my father, in the chalet he built for her in Switzerland during the time when his consultancy job with Pan American Airways took him frequently to Europe.

I used to look for feathers for her in Connecticut. I could usually find a striped blue-and-white one, forfeited by one combatant in a squabbling group of bluejays near the bird feeder, or a smooth gray one in the marsh grasses of the cove, left by one of the gulls who flew in and dropped clams on the rocks of the seawall to break them and get the food inside. Sometimes, though not often, a wisp of mottled speckle-brown down from a partridge or a pheasant's breast would be left on the lawn, or a slick greasy-looking black trophy feather from a visiting crow. Many years later, when we had guinea hens on the farm in Vermont, my mother liked the salt-and-pepper of their silly ruffed-up neck feathers, and once I found for her a brilliant gold-and-green curl, only about six inches long, from the end of a peacock's tail. It looked like a new spring fern, barely unfurled, but with a priceless, unblinking indigo eye.

"Feeding the birds is also a form of prayer," my mother has said to me from time to time, quoting Pope Pius XII, forever her favorite among the Pontiffs because he loved wild birds. My mother has always kept a part of herself in reserve, has always maintained a monastic quality somewhere in her life and spirit even during the busiest of family times. Throughout my childhood she kept, and still keeps at this writing, a carved wooden statue of Saint Francis by her window, with a bird in one of his hands and the other hand lifted in blessing. Behind the saint the chickadees outside my mother's window hop from branch to branch in a white pine much taller than the house, teeming with life.

In the summer of 1989, when it was clearly not going to be possible much longer for my mother to return to Switzerland because of her age and failing health, my husband and I traveled to see her there, with our children. It was at the end of what was to be her last summer in Europe, although none of us knew it at the time. My husband took the measurements of the house there, and during the following winter he had another chalet built on our farm in Vermont, similar but with some American adaptations. The fireplace in Vermont, for instance, is big, with a spacious brick hearth that opens onto the floor.

When the furniture from Switzerland eventually was to be moved into my mother's "Vermont Chalet," as she called it, a friend who knew her very well went over to pack up everything that seemed valuable, or necessary to her well-being. (A few minimal furnishings were left for friends and family members who might be traveling in Switzerland, before the house was sold.) The job was carefully accomplished, and the Swiss furniture arrived intact, along with the dishes, paintings, books, and Swiss handicrafts with which my mother had filled her summer home. Nothing that her friend thought might be important to my mother, however humble, was overlooked.

When the Swiss furniture arrived in Vermont, looking shaken and unsettled at first in its new surroundings, I happened to open a drawer in a great ancient armoire that had been used originally, my mother thought, to hold communion vessels and other sacramental necessities in a church vestry. Amidst the Michelin maps and candle stubs and various household tools my parents had used during their Swiss life, I found an odd rectangular and almost flat package. It seemed to be made mostly of paper towels, folded over and over, around something that appeared to have substance, but no weight at all. I unwrapped the package very slowly, thinking I might eventually see a piece of precious lace, or some other dainty European antique that my mother had treasured in Switzerland. Instead what I found was a sheaf of feathers, brown and gray and white and of earth-toned multicolors, collected for thirty years in Alpine forests and meadows. They spilled out softly, revealing themselves with the light unfolding of a painted fan, into my open hand.

Even to this day, many of the Christmas cards that come to my mother's house have paintings of angels on them, and she keeps and studies these many months after the holiday. She appears to be drawn in and enchanted by the formal grace of the interwoven feathers, and amazed by the gilded heaviness of the pinions.

"But how can they manage?" she asks, of an especially burdensome pair on the Metropolitan Museum's Angel of Annunciation. It is hard to imagine, but as she studies these paintings I wonder if maybe, somehow, my mother can imagine having wings. She is so silent, for so long, and she stares and stares. Is she trying, as hard as she can, to think her way into the body of the angel? And does she ever succeed, and get there? Can she feel the muscles pulling against the great feathered weight, like a backpack of spreading, eagerly stretching muscles and tendons? Is there a never before experienced sensation, for my small and elderly mother, of tremendous power and inevitable heavenward thrust? Or does she think her way into an element she already knows, and rest there, in a familiar grace?

8
Our Part of Connecticut

✳ ALTHOUGH I like to imagine that I grew up in a house made completely of stone, our home was really just another outsize, mock-Tudor structure made mostly of stucco, slate, and wood, like many others in the area. These early-twentieth-century fortresses along the shore had been built long before the commuter trains and the highways created the suburbs of New York City in the 1940s and 1950s. Thirty years before we came, our part of Connecticut had been "the country," and the big homes built there were weekend and vacation retreats for wealthy New Yorkers. Their winter addresses might be Gracie Square or Gramercy Park, but their summer estates bordered Long Island Sound on tracts of former farmland, like so many fiefdoms surrounding the city.

I was born at the close of World War II in 1945, and I grew up when the original owners of the weekend estates were dying out, and their property was being sold to new owners, or split up for suburban development. The farms, too, were disappearing from our part of Connecticut, leaving nothing of themselves behind but a few farmstands selling pumpkins and apple cider in the fall, along the Old Post Road. This was Route 1, running from Norwalk to Darien to Greenwich to Stamford and on into the mysteries of Port Chester and Rye, two towns

whose very names rolled with a dark and glamorous sound off
the lips of postwar Connecticut teenagers. These towns, unlike
ours, belonged to the state, and by association, to the city, of
New York.

In my teens, in the early 1960s, my friends and I could
drive to a place in Port Chester and buy spareribs on Friday
nights, and maybe beer, too, if somebody in the crowd was
older than the rest, or had a credible fake ID. Connecticut was
notoriously strict and punitive about underage drinking, even
in those days, but New York, if you knew where to go, was
different. If we wanted to try a more upscale corruption than
Port Chester offered, we could take a train to Grand Central
Station, walk around the block to meet a friend "under the
clock" at the Biltmore Hotel, offer up an older sister's passport
as identification, and order glasses of wine. The waiters at the
Biltmore would usually serve us, although they sometimes left
the table muttering.

In my early years, though, I had no interest in wine or
spareribs, no interest in New York. I was happy with life in our
Connecticut stone house, with its big oak door, its multiple
stories and stairways, its dark furniture and its wide-board
wood floors. I liked the closed-in, secret places: a pungent
cedar closet on the third floor; my mother's book-lined writing
room on the second; a cool and musty tool room down in the
basement that smelled in a greenish way of flowerpots and
faucets. I liked the free and light-loving places, too: the square
porches open to the cove and the sunsets, the high windows
full of trees and sky.

I was satisfied with the dimensions and conditions of my
home and family, with the openings and closings of doors, of
moods, of complex interweaving temperaments, familiar as the
ebb and flow of tides on the Sound.

Because of my father's instinct for concealment and seclusion, perhaps, there was on our property a permanent sense of quiet erosion from formality to disorder, a slow, gentle, and subversive fall from the standards of grander times. There was an old tennis court, for instance, with a chain-link fence all around it but no net or posts, and young maple trees growing up where the service line would be. Near it, marking the far end of the driveway, were two pillars of stone and mortar, and on each one a lion's head, their black paint peeling away. Outside the house there was a circular gravel driveway which we children often raked ourselves, in order to keep it smooth for cars and to earn money from our parents. This was one of the jobs I could do, unlike mowing the lawn or cutting brush, tasks left to the older children. In the center of the driveway there was a circle of earth, carefully edged with concrete, once a traffic island with plantings, now a formless tangle of shrubbery. While I raked I also noticed the rhododendrons that had been planted around the outer edge of the driveway, a formal curve of shrubs with their long curled sticky leaves and their big white unscented blossoms, backed up against the forest of brambles and vines that my father had allowed to grow up behind them, blocking the view from the cove.

There were pockets of horticultural order here and there, most of them near the house. There was one delicate Japanese maple tree, no taller than my lilac bushes are now in Vermont. It had thin, pointed, deep red leaves, and it spread its graceful branches in ceremonial elegance just to the side of the path leading to the front door. Crocus, narcissus, and daffodils bloomed at the edge of our small, sloped lawn in early spring, and shady places below the oak and maple trees were thick with myrtle. The tiny, deep blue flowers blossomed underfoot all through the woods, but fell off their stems immediately when I tried to pick them. There was a dogwood tree that bloomed outside my window every year. Its white flowers had stained pink hearts that one of our nurses told me were left over from the blood of Jesus, but I didn't believe it.

The animals liked the unkempt wildness of our land. There were geese, herons, and ducks in the marsh, and there were raccoons in our woods, along with box turtles, snakes, and sometimes deer. The deer then seemed magical, not the commonplace pests of today who raid gardens and spread Lyme disease to the families of Fairfield and Westchester counties. Our deer were timid, infrequent guests, half concealed by dusk or mist, to me as haloed and unexpected as angels. We considered ourselves lucky to catch sight of a doe stealing across a meadow in the early morning fog, or to have our neighbor show us a fawn he had seen when he climbed up on his tractor at the end of a summer afternoon, curled up at the edge of the field he was just about to mow. And my father took me outside at night once, much later than my usual bedtime, to watch the deer come drifting in, tentative and ephemeral, to a salt lick he had left for them in the woods.

My father liked to take all of us out together to see natural phenomena at night: a flood, a storm, a skunk near the woodpile, a sky full of shooting stars. He stood close enough to me so that I could lean back against his leather jacket in the dark, and feel his heart beating. We stood in the clearing in the middle of the night, my family and the deer family together, all of us at the same time hidden and revealed.

Jon was there, the oldest and the quietest of all the brothers, smiling his secret, closed-mouth smile. Jon has never said more than was necessary to any situation, all his life, so that when he does speak his words mean more to me, and give me more, than other people's words do. This has remained true for fifty years.

Jon and I traveled together to be with our brother Land in the summer of 1996, just after the sudden death of Land's new wife, Libby. We arrived late at night at the log cabin where the bride and groom had been married only three months earlier, on a sunny afternoon near the bank of Montana's Big Blackfoot River. It was dark on the highway as Jon and I drove from the airport, and dark in among the tall pines of the old dirt road along the river, and my thoughts were also very dark. Why should this happen to Land, who was so happy in his new marriage? Why should it happen to anybody? How could life be so unfair? We parked by the wooden fence, and opened the door of the car and got out, and then Jon cleared his throat, and said to me one word,

"Stars."

I looked up at once to see a sky brilliant and full, with all the constellations in their places, and the whole bowl of the universe was so much more deeply illuminated than my understanding that my mind quieted. Jon and I greeted Land, hugging him tightly, and we all talked together for a while. Then we said good night, and I went upstairs and slept until morning, with Jon in the room across the hall. I dreamed that night of Libby, smiling in the darkness, hanging out the stars.

Jon and Land shared a big bedroom on the third floor when we were growing up, and Scott had a smaller one nearby. In each of these third-floor bedrooms, as well as the small guestroom that became for a while the home of our father's mother's brother, our great-uncle from Detroit, our father had installed a long, thick rope that could be used for climbing out the window in case of a fire. I envied the brothers these ropes, but most of all I envied them the third-floor bathroom, with its closed-in glass shower stall. It looked like an enormous aquarium, empty of water but full of possibilities, a place where Jon, if he caught one, could have kept a small whale.

They did not keep whales, but my brothers had snakes, for a while, in cages and aquariums on the Ping-Pong table in the big room that Jon and Land shared. Sometimes the snakes got out and slithered around the house, frightening guests or the long-suffering family assistants, or irritating Martha, who lived with us for many years as a cook, but was usually safe in her own wing of the house, above the kitchen. Depending on the season, somebody might have a turtle temporarily, a box turtle or a delicate painted turtle, but these were released in local woods or ponds before long. There was a time when we all had mice, and I was very fond of my guinea pig, Milky, who stayed with me long enough to have a litter of very ugly babies. When she got a case of mange, Scott cured her.

In summer, ivy and honeysuckle vines climbed up the sides of our house, clinging to the stones that framed the foundation and cornered the porches overlooking Scott's Cove, and to the gutters and the drainpipes. Anne in her two blond braids, almost to her waist, showed me how to bite the tips off the yellow-white honeysuckle blossoms, and to suck out tiny sips of sweetness from them. There was not quite enough sweetness to be worth the effort, but it was interesting to try, like the small, strange taste of mint, or the slight squeak and heady breath of chives picked and chewed out of boredom and inertia on summer afternoons.

Anne also showed me how to climb above the ivy and honeysuckle vines, up the porch drainpipe, barefoot, as she did, in order to get to our bedrooms, which were close to our parents' room on the second floor. This was strictly forbidden —the pipes were flimsy, and if we fell we could hit either the porch or the granite steps that led up to it, risking serious injury. Anne taught me how to make the climb stealthily anyway, putting most of my weight on the stones by using my toes like monkey fingers to grip them, then swinging myself up quickly over the pewter-colored sheet-metal gutter of the family porch roof, and tiptoeing silently across the flat stucco covering it until I reached my own window. It was a skill that came in handy when we were in our teens, but one we never exercised when our father was at home.

Most of the time when he was at home, my father's office contained him comfortably and predictably, like a hermit's cabin deep in the woods, or like the well-designed cockpit of a small airplane. The office was a small square space on one side of the family porch on the first floor. It had been built as a twin to my mother's moonflower porch on the other side, but it was much more self-defended, with thick arched windows in the places where the moonflower porch had screens, and with less easy access to the outdoors.

The room had a single bed under the window, with a Hudson Bay blanket spread out upon it, and there were usually manila envelopes and boxes of onionskin typing paper arranged in piles on it, too. His desk and chair were in a corner, both smaller than might have been expected for a man his size, though this was typical of my father. He required a certain amount of room for himself and no more, and he didn't like to waste things: toothpaste or toilet paper, money or detergent, time or space.

His desk faced the door, not the view. Above it on the wall there was a small oil painting of an orchard in bloom, which I am sure my father told me he had painted himself, though I don't know when. There were shiny pink blossoms in the painting, and a great many little shiny green leaves. If I came into his office from the living room I could see his face immediately, and the whole of the cove behind him through the arched window, calm and wide and full of sky. My father spent a great deal of time outdoors, he said, but when he came inside he did not necessarily want to look at the scenery through a pane of glass, or to have it looking at him, so he worked with his back to the window. "You can *walk* to a view," he would argue.

In planning a home anywhere in the world, whether it was Connecticut or Switzerland, my father was never quite as interested in what we could see out through the windows as in who might be able to see us, looking in.

There was one door to my father's office from our living room, and another door in the stone side wall, too. This door could open onto the family porch, but it almost never did. It was painted gray, and it was always locked, and it looked anyway as if it was made of steel, like the door to a vault. Once, though, it opened without warning, when the rest of the family was sitting on the family porch next to the office. I thought at the time that we must be making too much noise, and that our father was opening the door to lecture us into trembling silence, and chase us away.

But it wasn't like that at all. We heard a push of air and a scrape like the sound of furniture being moved, and then the stone itself seemed to give way, and there before us was our father, in his tan chinos and his blue shirt, framed on all sides by rock, like a roadside statue of the Madonna. He was smiling at us, beaming as if delighted that we were having such a good time. His sudden arrival in our midst, not to mention his mood, were both so unexpected that for an instant I couldn't believe he had simply opened his office door to make his appearance. I thought he must have broken through the wall.

My mother had a flower garden, away from the house, on a high spot far from the water. There was a collection of rosebushes with metal tags, and a circle of annual beds set next to a rocky wall. There were two stone pillars, forming a kind of gate in the wall, and on top of each one half a giant shell, like the one on which Venus appears in the Botticelli painting. I hold in my memory a vision of my mother in that garden, kneeling with her back to me, planting pansies. I can see the cove at low tide, between interlaced tree branches, behind her dark head.

The most fascinating thing for me in my mother's garden was not a flower or a plant, but an immovably huge, verdigris-covered ship's bell that was a kind of central ornament in the informal circle of flower beds she tended, the way a statue or a fountain might be central to a much larger and grander garden. This bell, which never tolled, was too large in diameter for my arms to reach around it, and too heavy for me to move it in any direction, up, down, or sideways. I have been told that the man who owned the house before my parents had a collection of naval artifacts. This one may have been too heavy to move when he left. I don't know which ship the bell originally came from, or at what foundry it was cast, or why at the end of its sea-voyaging it had landed on a pile of rocks among our rosebushes. It looked lost there, as if it had materialized out of some midshipman's storm-racked fever dream, hundreds of pounds of cast bronze cut loose by wind and weather, float-ing off through thin air like a milkweed seed on an autumn breeze.

Wherever it had come from, the bell could not be budged, at least not by me. I often shoved against it, pushing as hard as I could in an effort to move it even a small fraction of an inch in any direction. I wanted to see what was under it, rocks or dirt or a mass of pale worms that would squirm in a repulsive way and make me shudder when I exposed them to the sun-light. But I could not displace the bell by even a millimeter, so I would lie down on my stomach on the rocks and try to squint underneath, looking for secrets. I thought I might find a clapper, at least, hanging there in dumb cobwebbed obscurity. I wanted to hear the bell ring. But I could see nothing but darkness underneath, and I could smell nothing but a cool, metal mustiness, the forlorn sour scent of a musical instrument no longer in service, voiceless as an abandoned bassoon.

Eventually, out of this impression of darkness and coolness, my imagination created beneath the mute motionless ship's bell a story that explained its presence in my family's garden. Beneath the bell, I decided, there was a hollow, ever-descending well, long since drained of water, a tube of emptiness below our garden and below our home, with its far end fatally deep and distant, most likely in China. The bell, I concluded, had been placed on top of the horrible hole by my father, who had recognized and neutralized this danger to his family as soon as he had purchased the Connecticut property. He had moved the bell with his bare hands, I was sure, had moved it the very first day, to cover this long, cold hole in our flower garden, and ensure our safety. He was familiar with all the dangerous holes of the universe, I reasoned, and his job as I understood it was to protect his children from falling into any of them.

My father outdoors was defined for me by his work shirts, his khaki trousers, his kerosene cans, his handsaws, and his sawhorses, and indoors by his green erasers and his penknife and his pencil shavings. He liked to sharpen pencils with a knife, not a pencil sharpener. The wooden ends of his pencils did not taper neatly to a leaded point, like the ones I used in school. Instead they were carved into an ugly stub from which a quarter inch of pencil lead protruded, so long a lead that if it had been my pencil I would surely have broken it, but he didn't. He didn't like pencil sharpeners, and he didn't like paper napkins, either. He never used one at the dinner table. He said it was a waste of paper, and that he preferred his pocket handkerchief. Anne and I both thought this was unsanitary, to say the very least.

I noted his eccentricities, as I noted the uncertainties of his temper and mood, and I had many opinions about these things when I was living with my father. I often laughed at him behind his back, and I sometimes fumed in tears and fury, alone in my room, and was sure that it was all his fault. I believed he was unjust, demanding, and difficult, just as often as I believed he was the strongest, most exciting, most intelligent, and most truthful person in the world. I took for granted that he would protect me from all dangers, from floods and blizzards to tooth decay and television. I knew that I could count on him, always, even though he could not always count on me.

I disagreed with him about television. It held no terrors. All I ever watched was *Howdy Doody,* anyway, and who could be afraid of Buffalo Bob? I knew that my own family would never have TV, and understood from my father's lectures that it was a bad influence upon young minds, and that it would be better for us all to be reading books. I read plenty of books, but I sneaked over to the neighbor's house as often as I could anyway to watch *The Howdy Doody Show.* I could see that it was useful to be able to fly an airplane, change a tire, or shoot a gun, in the appropriate circumstances. I did not understand why it was so terrible to eat candy or unenriched white bread, read *Dick Tracy* comics, or watch television. I thought my father was, too often, both unfair and absurd.

But I stood at the front door of our house with my sister once, confronting a man who had arrived and knocked while the family was having lunch. I did not hear what the visitor, a thin young man I did not recognize, had said to Anne, but I heard her cry out and step back into the doorway, and I saw her shut the door hard and fast, heavy as it was, in the stranger's face. Then, immediately, I heard my father's running footsteps behind us. He opened the door again and stepped outside with the stranger, putting his hands on Anne's shoulder and on mine as he passed us, urging us back into the house. But before we swung the door shut again, I saw that he was walking down the path beside the young man, and that he had put a hand on the stranger's shoulder, too, and was talking to him gently and at length.

On this occasion his face did not have the grim, closed-down look on it, the look fateful to duck hunters. Instead I saw kindness on it, and was confused to see that expression at that time; kindness and the open, loose-featured patience with which he approached nervous dogs or very small children. He didn't have the cold eyes and stern expression of the family disciplinarian on his face that day, or the grim, besieged look of the Defender of Our Property. Instead he looked the way I saw him look again once, years later in another house, gazing quietly down upon a stray bird that had just flown at full speed into our kitchen windowpane, and lay stunned and twitching in my father's hand.

It turned out that the visitor was one of the "Pretenders," as Anne used to call them, a reference to Charles Stuart, the "Bonnie Prince Charlie," who tried and failed to become King of England during Hanoverian times. This man was one of the dozen or more confused, sad individuals who have touched our lives now and then, over the years. Each one tells a different story, each repudiates the stories of all the others, yet all share the same obsession. Every one of them is convinced that he and nobody else is the Lindbergh baby who died, our own lost brother, Charles.

9
The Lost Baby

✳ I KNEW almost nothing about the kidnapping while I was growing up. I don't remember ever hearing my parents talk about it together, not even once. And although my mother spoke to me about the first child in our family occasionally, over the years, my father never did. I can imagine how much this baby must have meant to my father, who had been raised as an only child. This was the very first one of us, the son that he and my mother had made together in the youth of their marriage, a baby born fresh and new into the adventure that was their life together. I can imagine what it must have meant to him to have this child, this Charles, this namesake. I can even imagine, at times, what it must have meant to lose the child, in the way that he was lost. I know that the loss was immeasurable and unspeakable because, I, too, long after my father's death, lost a child almost exactly the same age. I understand why, in all the time I knew my father, I never heard him say this brother's name.

Our first brother's life and death was not a subject of conversation among the siblings, either, as we grew up and lived our lives together in the family where he should have been the oldest son. With us, there was perhaps a feeling of constraint caused by our parents' silence, though it was certainly not a question of being forbidden to talk about him. I think most of all there was a common understanding among the siblings, during my growing-up years, that this baby, like the 1927 flight to Paris, was part of an era that had nothing to do with us.

I have a visual memory of my brother's story, though it is not a private vision. It is made up of the dark images of old press photographs, and the jerky black-and-white newsreel footage from the 1930s that occasionally flashed across the Pathé Newsreel retrospectives I saw at the movie theater or in junior high school history programs. The kidnapping was not part of my daily life, but it was a moving shadow in the background of my experience nonetheless, another piece of the past that both was and was not mine.

From the first time I heard of it, I thought of the central tragedy itself, the death of my brother, as an accident. This may have been the way the story was presented to me by my mother. It was certainly the assumption she herself held, and revealed in her diaries from the 1930s. I did not see these diaries until they were published in book form, long after I had grown up and had children of my own, but it must have been our family position that the child's death was an accident, because I cannot think of it in any other way. Even as I grow older, and move as frequently outside my family circle as within it, encountering the "Lindbergh kidnapping" now as an event in American history, like the dropping of the atom bomb on Hiroshima, or the assassination of President Kennedy, it has never occurred to me that there was a murder victim in my family.

I still do not understand fully what the "Lindbergh kidnapping" story means to other people, those who have no inside view at all, and have only read about it. I try to think of other shocking historical events that might be comparable, events that start with one human victim, and then balloon into some enormity where the individual is lost. When I grope for meaning I come up with, for instance, the assassinations in the 1960s, the Kennedys and Dr. Martin Luther King, Jr., but it isn't the same. These were men, world leaders, not babies. I sometimes think of Anne Frank, another innocent child, but she, too, had a position of her own in the world, and left a voice, heartbreaking and eloquent, to speak her own words, in her own diaries, after she was gone. But this baby, my brother, what did he leave? Who speaks for him? What did his life mean?

I experience a kind of numb bewilderment every time I encounter a casual public reference to my brother's life and death. I know that there must be a common social context in which other people can place these references, but I just draw a blank. For instance, when I saw the film *The Fisher King,* starring Robin Williams, there was a moment when an actor vamped across a theater stage in a woman's pink dress and a feather boa, and wailed, "I'm Anne Morrow Lindbergh. Where's my baaaaby?" I was startled, confused, wanted to ask someone what the scene meant to them. Is that funny? Is it sad? Does it provide historical context? Do most people who see it immediately understand something I never will, or is the scene as bizarre and meaningless for them as it is for me?

Recently when my son was watching the TV series *The Simpsons,* a character said, "I'm the Lindbergh baby—wah! wah! wah!" Benjamin asked me, "What's the Lindbergh baby?" I explained, not for the first time, what that old, sad story was, but then he asked me impatiently—he knew the history part —why the reference was on the show. I had no idea. I didn't get it. I don't think I ever will. At these times I feel like a foreigner in my own life, trying to read the subtitles in a language I can't master.

Eventually, through reading and research in my teens and

early twenties, I came to know as much as most other people did about the kidnapping and death of my brother, and about the arrest, trial, conviction, and ultimate execution of the man accused of the crime. And I continued to believe that the baby died because of a mistake, not as the result of a deliberate act of violence.

Somebody, I reasoned, was crazy and greedy and an avid reader of newspapers. This person or persons thought up what they believed to be a foolproof scheme to make money. They would take the well-publicized Lindbergh baby from his young parents by stealth, and hold him for ransom. The parents were rich, they would surely pay.

It must have seemed very simple, in the planning. Then when it came time to carry out the plan, there was so much risk and stress and fear involved, as well as a dark night and a struggling toddler, that the plan came to a disastrous end. The kidnapper lost his grip at the crucial moment, climbing down the ladder from the child's bedroom, and the baby was dropped, fatally. The body was buried hastily in the woods, the kidnapper fled and then tried to carry out the ransom plan anyway, but failed and was apprehended. The child died from a blow to the head, I knew, but I have willed myself all my life not to believe that the blow had been deliberate.

In my vision the kidnapping and death happen in a matter of seconds, during which the baby is not fully conscious. In my vision he passes from sleep to death so quickly that he never knows the difference between the two. He feels some discomfort, yes, at being disturbed in his slumber; he fights against it, he gets loose, he falls, he dies—immediately. There are no gaps in the sequence my mind has invented for this story, there are no terrors and there is no anguish for this baby, my brother. He never feels fear or pain. He never wakes and panics. He never cries out for his mother. It is all over before he can feel a thing.

I did not know whether this was a likely scenario, and did not want to know if it wasn't. It is the only way I have ever been able to think about the death of my brother Charles, a child not yet two years old. He died for no reason, on a night long ago, when he was just minding his own baby business, sleeping in his crib. He became a sensation, a court case, a capital punishment law (since repealed), a media phenomenon, the subject of a dozen books or more, and a source of nightmare anxiety, for a time, for parents and children all over the world. But the little boy himself was just a baby, a real flesh-and-blood child, sleeping in his pajamas, as real as my child or yours. He is remembered around the world not for his life but for his death, and his death made no sense at all.

As I get older I think of my brother Charles more and more often as a real child, rather than a piece of history. With help from my mother's diaries and from my own life, I have been able to reclaim him a little, imagining his life and returning him to his family, out of his sensationalized and distorted "story." I can do this partly because he is connected in my mind and heart with my own son Jonathan, who died at the same age. Jonny too died in the night, and I, like my mother before me, was apart from my son during his last moments. I too thought that the baby was safely asleep in his crib. My son died of a seizure related to infant encephalitis, just a few weeks before his second birthday, while he and I were staying at my mother's new house in Connecticut. When I went to wake him up in the morning, I found him dead.

After we had called the local emergency squad—although the body was stiff and blue, and it was clear that Jonny had been dead for several hours—we notified the police, and the family, and the funeral home. Then, because she insisted upon it, my mother and I went and sat together with Jonny's body, in two chairs, next to the crib where he had gone to sleep the night before.

I really did not want to sit there, and as I sat I wanted, several times, to scream and run from the room—anywhere, everywhere—but I didn't do it. My mother had told me that the most important thing to do now was to go and sit in the room with the baby, just sit there quietly with him, and not do anything else but that, as long as his body was still there. I believed her, as I have always believed her, and so I sat.

"I never saw my child's body, after he died," she said to me, sitting beside me in my chair and beside Jonathan's still body in his crib. "I never sat with my son this way."

Then I understood her, and I had at that moment a rush of sheer, self-congratulatory, all-engulfing family pride. It was a kind of insanity, my feeling pride at that time. This was a moment for personal maternal agony, nothing else. But I was proud all the same, proud that my child and I had given this quiet time to my mother, who had not been able to have it when her own son died. His body, after it had been identified by his father, his pediatrician, and his nurse, had been cremated, and my father then scattered his ashes from the air. I knew the story, had known it all my life, but on the day of my own son's death I was, for the first time, part of it. For the first time, it was absolutely real.

For a little while, as I sat with my dead son and his quiet grandmother, this sense of reality was the strongest feeling in me, heady and nostalgic and as dizzying to the senses as a lilac bush that I once saw blooming unexpectedly out of season, in my neighborhood in a foreign city, calling me back to my country and my home.

Although it was brief, and very strange, the feeling lasted

long enough that I can recall it out of the turmoil of that
terrible morning, out of my own shock, my growing sense of
prickling disorientation, out of the gathering deep rumble of
what would soon be my madwoman's, mad-mother's roaring,
uncontainable grief.

Other parents who have lost their children will understand
the way this grief, when fully developed, changed me completely. From then on, it was as if my life had been cleaved:
everything before the day of Jonny's death belonged to one
person, and everything afterward to another. But the grief had
not yet begun to grow, and I knew when I heard my mother's
words, the morning of my son's death, that the tornado devel-
oping within me would not come out, not yet. No matter how
much I wanted to run, flee, shriek, explode, tear the world
apart, I would not do it, not yet. I would sit quietly with my
son, and with my mother, instead, and I would be proud that
we were sitting together, my mother and I, sitting quietly next
to that crib in that house, not with one dead baby, but with
two.

Monday, May 23, 1932

As I walked into his room, before I looked at everything, every-
thing came back. I looked at his toys, the rooster, the Swedish horse,
the music box, spools and crayons, the little blue stool, his cart of
blocks, my scrapbook.

The Johnson powder tin, sweet to smell. The pictures I tacked up
on the wall for him, the white table and chair. Then the bureau
drawers—each one so full of him. There was a new poignantly
personal thing in each drawer . . . mussed and crushed under blan-
kets, the little blue knitted jacket he wore over his sleeping suit when
he came down to play every night. I put my face in it . . .

Anne Morrow Lindbergh, *Hour of Gold, Hour of Lead*

(New York: Harcourt Brace Jovanovich, 1973)

When I read my mother's words, from diaries written more than sixty-five years ago, I close the book and I see my own Jonathan's light blue snowsuit, feel the sweet heft of Jonny in it, smell his flushed neck and silky hair, know his light hand on my arm as I hold him and he, too, holds me, as babies do, in the dance of reciprocity with their mothers: breast to mouth, hand to arm, heart to heart. I can see the clothing that he left behind for me to find after he was gone, remember how the sight of it flooded me each time with love and pain, bringing his presence and his absence together invincibly, many months after his death, when one tiny white sock, still warm, tumbled out with the rest of the laundry from the drier.

The two lost babies in our family, separated by more than fifty years, remain individual, unique: each clear and beloved by his own particular family, each belonging to his own particular place in time—Charles, in 1932, the brother I recognize intimately from photographs even though I never knew him; Jonny, my own boy in 1985, the grandson with whose sudden death my mother could sit quietly at last, in her own home. And yet, although each boy lived his life unconnected with the other, there has been a blending and sharing of experience for the two mothers. When Jonny died, one of the boundaries between mother and daughter dissolved, and through the unexpected opening each of us was able to move, from time to time, to meet the other, sometimes bringing comfort, sometimes simply sharing pain.

"That was my baby," my mother said on one of her disoriented days, a year or two ago, pointing at a picture of Jonathan that stood on the mantelpiece at the house of an old family friend. The friend was distressed, and looked quickly over at me, but I did not protest, and could not disagree. After all, whenever I read her diaries from 1932, written thirteen years before I was even born, I walk with her into Charles's nursery, and I look at his toys and his blankets, and I bury my face in his clothing. I am there with her completely, sixty-five years ago, and because of Jonny, her lost baby is my lost baby, too.

In our household, in the 1980s, Jonathan had two older sisters who remembered and grieved for him, as his parents did. They too missed the look and smell and feel of Jonny every day, ached for his bright blue eyes, his smile, the silly, chuckling sound of his baby laughter. But my parents lost their son Charles when he had no sisters or brothers. None of the children who came afterward had any firsthand knowledge of the first one, none of them could miss him, or think of him in a personal way. I have wondered if the lack of connection between the lost child and the others made my mother's life easier or more difficult in the busy child-rearing years that followed, or whether her life simply split in half, the way mine did, with the life of that first motherhood as far removed from the current life as if separated by an ocean, on a shore that became too distant to recall or even to imagine in detail anymore, except in dreams.

I have always been glad, on behalf of all six of her children, that my mother was pregnant with the second when she lost the first. It links us together, whether we knew it or not, and it gives me comfort for my mother's sake to know that before our brother Charles was gone, our brother Jon was already on his way.

My own second son, Benjamin, did not know his lost brother, and when I told him about Jonny's life and death, I chose my words carefully. Ben was born two years after Jonny died, and was himself delivered with a stillborn twin. Healthy and exuberant, he has been curious, at one time or another, about his two almost-brothers, the twin and Jonny. I do not talk about them very often, because I do not want Ben to feel the importance of his own babyhood is compromised, squeezed between two deaths. The other babies do not really belong in his story, even though they were a part of mine. I want him to be free of his parents' past, just as my parents wanted me to be free of theirs, even though I know this is not really possible for any of us.

The first time Ben asked me about Jonny, I told him the story in a simple way, while he listened thoughtfully, and then I prepared myself for his response. Ben turned to me at once, with a radiant smile.

"Boy, Mom, are you ever lucky!" he said. "After all that, you got me!"

If my mother had spoken to me about the kidnapping and the lost brother, during my childhood, I would have said much the same thing. Our mother was *our* mother, exclusively. She was mine, and Jon's and Land's and Anne's and Scott's. How happy she must be to have us, and so many of us, I sometimes thought. Whatever her troubles may have been in the past, they were all over now. What a lucky woman!

There have been a number of people, in addition to the young man who appeared at our door in the 1950s, who believe that the baby survived, somehow—a mysterious switch with another child, a Mafia plot, a secret, unfathomably complicated series of misfortunes that resulted in the "real" Lindbergh baby growing up in the wrong family, in California, or in Connecticut, or in Maine, or even, in one case, in Bombay. I have over the years had letters from several of the men who believe that they are my long-lost brother, or from these men's relatives. Some of them have written lengthy typed communications, passionate if not logical, including many pages of "proof" in the form of photocopied poems, articles, and miscellaneous quotations. One of them sent me an incoherent collection of cut-and-pasted words from magazines and newspapers, a concoction that looked eerily like the ransom notes from old movies. One sent me an envelopeful of bitter accusations against another Lindbergh baby claimant, whom he wished to expose as a fraud.

The most active currently is a man who still sends Hallmark greeting cards from California, including pictures of his family, at Christmas and Easter. The Californian has a persuasive manner, and once brought my mother's New York attorney out of a conference by giving this message to his secretary: "Mr. Lindbergh is on the telephone long distance." When he writes, he uses very small, precise handwriting, although his spelling is sometimes unusual and he often avoids the use of the upper case.

I get letters about the kidnapping from about a half dozen different people each year, some claiming to be my lost brother, others to be the child of my brother, and to have heard him confess his identity on his deathbed. Still others claim to have some "special" or "secret" knowledge about the kidnapping. Not long ago, at a book signing for one of my new children's books, a man in his late seventies made his way through the group of children and parents to insist that I read three typed pages ("a signed affidavit!" he said, repeatedly) claiming that he, at the age of fourteen, had seen my father with Bruno Richard Hauptmann, the man convicted of the crime, in a shack in the woods in the 1930s. I did not tell this man that my parents had been flying together over Asia at the time he indicated, mapping out air routes and being photographed and entertained in foreign cities. Instead I listened to him for a while, and then wrote down the name and address of the same family attorney, should he wish to contact him.

The letters I receive come from all over the United States and from many foreign countries as well. My favorite "Lindbergh baby" letter was from someone in India, written in a cheerful and buoyant tone, with a kind of Publisher's Clearing House optimism. "Yes, Reeve!" it begins. "The search for your brother is finally over!" The writer says that while everyone around him believes he is a native of Bombay, in fact he is Charles Lindbergh's lost son, who has undergone many medical and other unspecified transformations at the hands of his enemies, to disguise his identity. He apologizes for not having responded earlier to what he refers to as "your family's desperate attempts to contact me." He urges us all warmly "not to worry," that he is well and content after many hair-raising adventures since he left our family so many years ago, and ends with a polite message, "Please feel free to contact me at any time. Tell someone to wake me up, if required."

I am sometimes angry—Why doesn't this craziness ever stop?—but most often touched by these appeals—What could have happened to these people?—Where are their real families? Still, I have never written back to any of them, and never will, because I believe that to do so would be cruelly exploitive. But I am sorry that so many other people have attached their own misery to this piece of our family history.

I have heard scores of theories and speculations that have grown up around the story of this tragedy—that there were conspiracies and cover-ups, that the baby was killed by a jealous or deranged relative. Books, movies, lawyers' reputations have been built around some of these outrageous stories. Yet I have never doubted the truth of what must have happened. It was very simple, very brutal, and very fast. The speculations and the fantasies that arose around this event may be with us for a hundred years, but I believe that my brother's part in it lasted for only a few minutes.

I believe that the identification of my brother's body was accurate, not only because the records show that hair, bones,

teeth, and other identifying factors were verified by the author-
ities, but also because one of the people making the final
identification, along with the baby's pediatrician and his nurse,
was my father.

With all my powers of imagination brought to bear, I cannot
begin to imagine what my father felt when he made the identification of his own dead baby, his first, lost son. All the same I
am sure that the process itself as he went through it, every step
of the way, was scientific, thorough, and correct in every detail.
When he had finished his examination of the child's body,
there would have been no room left for doubt.

People have pointed out that my father must have been in a
state of deep shock and grief at the time, and perhaps would
not have been as accurate as he normally would be. But I think
the opposite is more likely. I think that the more shock and
grief my father felt, the more conscientiously he would have
pursued the task at hand, neglecting nothing, omitting nothing. He would have been going over his list, and over it, and
over it. He would be checking and rechecking, and checking
again. He might think, perhaps, that he was making sure that
his feelings did not interfere with his judgment, but in fact his
feelings, at white heat, would themselves illuminate and hone
his judgment to its finest point. His feelings would make it
possible for him to travel, fired by passions he would be hard
put to express in any other way, as far into accuracy and scientific detail as he could possibly go, as far as he could reach for
the truth, which would be his only comfort. To seek truth in
the tangible was not just something my father had learned to
do, as a farm boy, an engineer, a pilot. It was a statement of
faith, and as such it became the greatest strength he could offer
his family during the tranquil periods of our lives, and at the
moments of unspeakable disaster as well. That moment in
1932, when he identified the body of his first, dead son before

any of the rest of his children had yet been born, was certainly
the worst of all possible times for my father. It was at the same
time the truest and the most intimate measure of the father
he was.

10
Being the Airplane

✳ H E took us flying on Saturdays. It didn't happen every Saturday, of course. Still, I spent quite a few of my Saturday afternoons in the 1950s several thousand feet in the air over the state of Connecticut, flying with Charles Lindbergh.

I know that many people would yearn to have had the same experience, but as far as I was concerned, I was just sitting in the rear cockpit of a very small airplane, feeling a little sick to my stomach. I looked down at the forests and the fields and the houses and the roads below me from an intense, vibrating height and hoped that my father would not notice that I had cotton balls stuffed in my ears.

I think that my father wanted to share his love for the air and for airplanes with his growing family, the way sports-minded fathers took their children to ball games on Saturday afternoons, and taught them to play catch afterward. My father took his children to the airport, instead, and taught them to fly.

Though he was the pilot on these flights, my father did not own the airplane. It was a 65 horsepower Aeronca, with tandem cockpits, that he rented from a former bomber pilot whose name was Stanley Konecko. Stanley managed the airport, including the huge loaf-shaped hangar that served as a garage for repairs and maintenance to the aircraft, and he leased out the group of small planes tethered near the building like a fleet of fishing boats clustered around a pier.

It was Stanley, most often, who stood in front of the airplane and waited for my father to shout "ConTACT!" from the cockpit window, at which time Stanley gave the still propeller a hefty downward shove that sent it spinning into action, and started the plane shaking and shuddering on its way. The job of starting the propeller was simple, but perilous. My father had warned us many times about the danger of standing anywhere near a propeller in action. We could list almost as well as he did the limbs that had been severed from the bodies of careless individuals "in a split second" by a propeller's whirling force. Each time, therefore, that Stanley started the propeller I would peer through its blinding whir to catch a glimpse of any pieces of him that might be flying through the air. Each time I saw only Stanley, whole and smiling, waving us onto the asphalt runway with his cap in his hand and his hair blowing in the wind of our passing—the "propwash," my father called it.

My sister and my three brothers flew on Saturdays, too. The older ones were taught to land and take off, bank and dip, and even to turn the plane over in midair, though Land confessed that he hated this, it made him feel so dizzy. Scott remembers our father instructing him to "lean into the curve," as the plane made a steep sideways dive toward the ground. Scott was already off balance, leaning *away* from the curve, and hanging on for dear life. For my sister, our father demonstrated "weightlessness," by having the plane climb so sharply that for a second she could feel her body straining upward against the seatbelt that held her, trying to fight free, while our father shouted out from the front seat that one of his gloves was actually floating in midair.

"See the glove? See the glove?" He called to her over the engine noise, and explained at the top of his lungs that if this state of weightlessness could continue, everything inside the plane would go up in the air. My sister nodded, not speaking, because everything in her stomach was going up in the air, too, and she did not dare open her mouth.

My oldest brother, Jon, took to flying immediately, and eventually got a pilot's license, though he ended up joining the Navy and becoming a frogman, spending as much time underwater with an aqualung and a wet suit as he ever had spent in the air.

What Jon secretly yearned to do during the flying years, though, was to jump right out of an airplane altogether, with a parachute. Finally he had his chance, and told me about it afterward. He stood at the open door of the airplane with the parachute strapped to his back, wobbling back and forth at first, like a baby bird afraid to leave the nest. Then he jumped, fell about a hundred feet through the air, and only then pulled the cord that caused the chute to blossom around him like a great circular sail. Swaying under it, he floated toward the ground until he landed, fairly hard.

I listened to Jon's story with delighted astonishment. I have always been thrilled to the bone by both the style and the daring of my three brothers. My father, on the other hand, along with most of the other early aviators, was not impressed by Jon's eagerness, or by the growing enthusiasm for para-chute-jumping as a sport. Young daredevils like my brother could call it "skydiving" if they wanted to, but the aviation pioneers referred to it disgustedly as "jumping out of a perfectly good airplane." In their day, a pilot only jumped when he had to, if it was absolutely certain that the airplane was headed for a crash, and the parachute was his only hope for survival.

I was considered too young for aerial adventures, so I did

not get dizzy, or actually sick, or have to worry about whether my parachute would open. It was mostly the noise that gave me trouble. I have never shared other people's enthusiasm for loudness. I don't like the sudden sounds that make you jump with alarm, like the noises of fireworks and guns, or the endless ones that pound in your head so hard you can't think about anything else, like the commotion made by jackhammers and the engines of small airplanes. My sister felt exactly the same way; in fact, Anne was the person who showed me how to stuff cotton balls in my ears, secretly, for takeoff, when the engine noise was loudest, and for as long during the flight as we could get away with it.

Our father frowned upon the cotton balls. If he saw them, he would make us remove them. He claimed that they diminished the experience of flying, and were in any case unnecessary: the engine noise was not so terribly loud that one couldn't get used to it. He certainly had done so.

Our mother, who had also flown back in the early days, always told us that she loved her experience as a glider pilot best, because there was such extraordinary quietness all around her. In the absence of the usual aircraft engine noise, she could hear the songs of birds and sometimes even the trilling of insects, crickets or cicadas, on the grassy hillsides below. She said that because there was no noise, she could actually feel the power of air, the way it could push up under the wings of a glider and keep it afloat like a boat on water, with the strength of unseen currents. She talked about "columns of air," stretching like massive tree trunks between earth and sky. Just because you can't see the air doesn't mean there's nothing to it, she said. Most of the really important things in our lives are invisible, anyway.

When it was my turn to fly with my father, I sat in the back cockpit and enjoyed the view all around us while he, in the

The two Charles A. Lindberghs, C.A. Lindbergh and my father, Charles A. Lindbergh, Jr., about 1910. My father said that his father, a Minnesota attorney and U.S. congressman, was known as "the handsomest man in Little Falls."

1

An undated studio portrait of my grandmother Evangeline Lodge Land Lindbergh and my father.

2

Charles H. Land, my grandmother's brother, around 1960. "Uncle" lived in my father's household during my father's childhood and lived with us while we were growing up.

3

The famous photograph of my father at the time of the 1927 flight.

My parents in 1933, in Cartwright, Labrador. This was around the time of their flights together, charting air routes for the fledgling aviation industry.

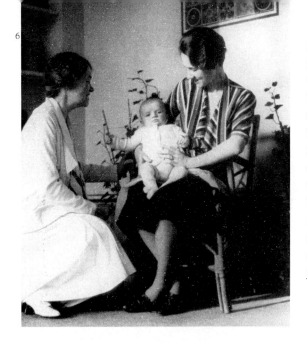

Elizabeth Cutter Morrow—or "Grandma Bee," as we knew her—and my mother, with my brother Charles A. Lindbergh III, who was also called Charles, Jr. It's always been important to me that my brother be remembered as the child that he was, not just as a headline.

My mother at Proto Praia, Santiago, Cape Verde Islands, in 1933. She told me that the years she spent flying with my father were some of the happiest times they spent together.

My brother Jon, my mother, and the
family dogs, Skean and Thor, at
Long Barn, Sevenoaks, England, in
January 1937. My parents rented
Long Barn from Harold Nicolson
and his wife, Vita Sackville-West.
Nicolson was the biographer of my
grandfather, Dwight Whitney
Morrow.

My father and Jon. Jon was very
much his father's son, independent
and completely at ease in the
natural world.

From left to right: Anne,
my mother, Jon, Scott (on
my mother's lap), and
Land, in 1943. As our family grew larger, my mother
stopped flying to stay
home with the children.

Me with my mother and my oldest sister, Anne. One of my earliest memories was looking at Anne's golden braids—one of our neighbors used to call her "the Queen of the Seven Braids" (even though she only had two).

Grandma Bee with her daughters and grandchildren in 1948. She would gather us together once a year for a family portrait. One year Jon and Land climbed a tree to hide from the photographer because they hated wearing suits and ties. I'm in the front row at the far right.

My father in 1949. I always thought of his navy blue pin-striped suit and gray fedora as his "going-away" and "coming-home" uniform.

13

14

My father, Jon, and me at Christmastime in Darien, 1953. Jon and my father used to toss me back and forth between them, a game that I loved.

In their later years together, my parents rediscovered Europe, especially Switzerland, where they built a house overlooking Lake Leman, near Vevey. My mother would return to Switzerland every summer for thirty years.

15

Jonathan Lindbergh Brown. Jonny, like my brother Charles, was only with us for a short time but remains an important part of our lives.

16

Benjamin Lindbergh Tripp. Ben told me how lucky I was to have him—and he's right.

17

Elizabeth and Susannah Lindbergh Brown, 1998.

18

Anne with her husband, Noel Perrin, at their home in Vermont in 1991.

My mother and Jon in 1997, not long after she turned ninety, at her home in Connecticut.

front cockpit, flew the plane. I had a duplicate set of controls in back, with rudder pedals, stick, and instruments, so that if I had been a true student pilot I could have flown the plane myself, when called upon to do so. But since I was too young to understand or even to reach most of the controls in my cockpit, I just watched them move as if by magic, with no help from me at all, in response to my father's direction and will.

It looked easy. The stick in front of me, exactly like the one in front of my father in the forward cockpit, looked a little like the gearshift on our Volkswagen. If the stick moved backward suddenly, though (toward me), it meant that my father had decided we were going to go up. What happened next was not at all like being in the Volkswagen. There would be a rushing in my ears, in spite of the cotton, and as I looked over my father's head through the front window of the aircraft I would imagine that we were forcing our way right into heaven, higher and higher through ever more brilliantly white banks of cloud. I sometimes daydreamed of bumping into angels, or startling Saint Peter at his pearly gates, or God Himself in His sanctuary.

But then, as I watched, my stick would point forward again, toward what I could see of the back of my father's neck over the top of the front pilot seat, with its trim fringe of gray hair and a khaki shirt collar. Then the airplane would nose down again, giving on all sides a cockeyed view of blue sky and wooded hillsides and little tiny roads with buglike cars creeping along them, so very slowly. I was always struck by the insignificance of the world we had left behind. Nothing looked real. Once I had climbed into the airplane, all of life seemed concentrated inside the loud space of it, shaking but steady, with my father's hand on the controls. We were completely self-sufficient, completely safe, rock-solid in the center of the sky.

I found it a little monotonous, frankly. My father did the

same things, and said the same things, loudly, over and over. I knew by heart that a pilot had to fly with a steady hand, with no sudden or jerky movements, just a little throttle here, a little wing dip there, always a light, even touch, always a calm approach. I knew all the stories about student pilots, those not already dismembered by propellers, who "froze" to the stick in a panic and would not let go, forcing the plane into a tragic nosedive. There was no room in my father's lessons for soaring like the birds, no swooping and circling. We just droned along, my father and me.

And then, one Saturday afternoon, we didn't. I don't remember exactly what made me understand there was something wrong with the airplane. I think there may have been a jerking sensation that repeated itself over and over. And I think that there was a huge stillness in the air, a silence so enormous that it took me a moment to realize that it was actually the absence of noise, not noise itself. The silence was there because the engine had stalled. Perhaps the most profound moment of silence occurred when my father realized that it was not going to start again, no matter what he did. We were in the middle of the sky, on a sunny afternoon over Connecticut, in a plane without an engine.

I don't think there was any drop in altitude, not at first. What I noticed was my father's sudden alertness, as if he had opened a million eyes and ears in every direction. I heard him say something sharp on the airplane's two-way radio to Stanley, down below, and I could hear the crackle of Stanley's voice coming back. I knew enough not to say very much myself, although my father told friends later that I asked him once, in a conversational way, "Are we going to crash?" And when he told this part of the story, the part where I asked that question, he would laugh.

I don't remember being afraid of crashing. In fact, I don't

remember fear at all, but I do remember excitement. At last something different was going to happen! I quickly took the cotton out of my ears, because my father was talking very seriously. He told me that he was looking for a good place to land. We would have to land, he explained, because the engine wasn't working, and we could not land at the airport because we were too far away to get there in time. (In time for what? I wondered.) He was looking for an open area to put the plane down, right below us somewhere. We were now over a wooded hillside, dotted here and there with cow pastures. It would have to be a cow pasture. He spotted one that looked possible, and circled down toward it.

There was nothing even remotely like a runway below us, and no room to spare. He would have to tip the plane sideways and slip it into the pasture that way, somehow righting it and stopping the momentum before it could hit any of the rocks at the four edges of the field. We circled lower and lower, barely clearing the treetops, and then he told me to put my head down between my knees.

"Hold on!" my father said.

I didn't see the landing, because my head was down, but I felt it, a tremendous series of bumps, as if we were bouncing on boulders, and then the plane shook and rattled to a stop. Then we took off our seatbelts, and opened the doors, and got out. I didn't see any cows in the pasture, but there were a bunch of people coming toward us from the road, and it looked as if one of them might be Stanley, from the airport. I was careful to stay clear of the propeller.

Nobody could figure out how we had landed safely. They had to take the plane apart to get it out of the pasture, a week or more after that Saturday afternoon. But my father and I got a ride back to the airport with Stanley, and drove home in plenty of time for dinner.

We didn't talk much on the drive home. My father seemed tired, and I was thinking. I had found out something about my father that afternoon, just by watching him work his way down through the air. I held on to the knowledge tightly afterward, and I still hold it to this day. I learned what flying was for him and for the other early aviators, what happened to him in an airplane and why he kept taking us up to try flying ourselves. As we came in through the trees, he was concentrating hard, getting the instruments set, trying to put us in the best possible position for a forced landing, but he was doing more than that, too. He was persuading and coaxing and willing the plane to do what he wanted it to do; he was leaning that airplane, like a bobsled, right down to where it could most safely land. He could feel it's every movement, just as if it were part of his own body. My father wasn't flying the airplane, he was *being* the airplane. That's how he did it. That's how he had always done it. Now I knew.

11
In a Pullman

✳ DESPITE the Saturday flights with my father, we rarely traveled by airplane. When we traveled as a family we went by car or, occasionally, and wonderfully, by train. We rode trains to visit both of our grandmothers, one in Detroit and the other, in the summertime, on the island of North Haven, in Penobscot Bay, off the coast of Maine. These trips were in themselves much more magical, mysterious, and satisfying to my imagination than any afternoon in the air over Danbury, Connecticut, with my father could ever be, even one that included a forced landing in a cow pasture.

The Detroit trip has concentrated itself in my memory into a series of fold-down beds in Pullman sleeping compartments. The very thought of these beds provided for weeks ahead of the journey a delicious mixed excitement of anticipations. There was above all the sheer novelty of sleeping in something so unlike my bed at home, something that did not stay in one place with a solid identity, fixed in its corner by the pale blue and oddly pimpled plaster walls of my own bedroom in Connecticut, just under the window where that branch of white dogwood bloomed every spring. Instead, this train bed was mobile. In fact it was doubly, almost dizzyingly mobile. It swung down nightly from the ceiling of a Pullman compartment that was itself in motion, en route anywhere from New Canaan to Kalamazoo, and then the bed revealed itself, fully laden with bedding made up clean and tight, ready for me to slide inside in a slim and tidy traveler's manner. I savored the sensation, as my small body in my clean nightgown (marked by the neat creases of a well-packed suitcase, thanks to my mother) slipped in between those sheets as smoothly as a folded letter slips into an envelope.

I liked the intimate anonymity of those beds, the way they were ready for me ahead of my time with them, then ready again for somebody else after I left them. I was a lover of hinged and continuous things, anyway, from the ironing boards attached to walls behind closet doors at the grandmothers' houses, to the miraculous rolls of cloth towels in the ladies' rooms at the railroad stations all across the nation. I never grew tired of watching those endless loops of institutional linen disappear, still grubby and wrinkled from the touch of my fingers, into their white dispensers, then emerge again instantly, clean and pressed. It was a joy to me that no matter how fast or how often I pulled at these rolls, even if I sidled up on them from around a corner or made a sudden rush at them from the sink when nobody was watching me, I could not thwart the process.

Traveling with my father in a Pullman car to Detroit, like traveling with him in an airplane, was an experience that felt completely safe because he was so unmistakably in control. Still, the trip was not without its anxieties and its hazards. I loved the top bunk, for instance, but more often slept in the bottom one. This was not only because others, older and stronger than I, had claimed it, but also because I harbored an unarticulated nervous dread that having folded down, the bed might just possibly fold up again, with me in it, while I slept. And although I was enchanted by the fittings of the compartment—the whiteness of the linens, the silvery sheen of the tiny sink in one corner and the answering gleam of the toilet in another—so brilliantly clean, polished like everything else to a sanitized metallic shine—there was again a kind of nervous horror each time I used the plumbing—What happened next? Did everything that swirled down into that shiny bright train-ride plumbing just keep on going into nowhere? Or did it appear again, on the tracks we rushed over so heedlessly, to disgust the inhabitants of the countryside? If so, why did my father not tell us about it? (Talk about punk design!) I chose not to ask. Pullman plumbing was as thrilling in its own way as the ladies' room towels in their infinite loops, and as precious to me in its ambiguities. All, all of this spoke to me in seductive, silvery, singing voices all along the way, rattling with the danger and rumbling with the romance of the rails.

I don't think I could have spared any time during the day to look out the windows, on these trips, because I can't remember a bit of the daytime scenery we must have passed on the way to Michigan. I do remember the lights we saw, at night. Unknown small railroad stations passed by us in the dark, appearing and then disappearing like sudden swarms of fireflies in our travelers' night. Sitting on the bottom berth with my brother Scott and my sister Anne, I tried with them to identify each town we passed before it was gone forever. Nothing one traversed with such speed could be permanent or recoverable, we knew: not the moment, not the place itself, nothing. On trains, even now, I have the same sense that whatever I pass is immediately and forever in the past, whether I am on a familiar line or in a foreign country: this barn, this house, this child on a bicycle, that horse tossing its head in a green meadow, those mountains in the distance, that one quick glimpse of a city street and all its traffic, today's lightening sky with cloud configurations particular to this very morning and no other, all are here together at once, now, with me, and then all are gone. Never again this conjunction, this moment. All gone forever. I wonder if that feeling is universal for travelers, or if it came to me from those first journeys, where my sense of place was limited to the familiarity of family members and the strange immediacy of the Pullman compartment so completely and yet so temporarily ours. We Lindberghs were everywhere and nowhere, all one family in time, while outside our moving window, lost in the vastness of other people's America, town after town rushed by us, named and nameless, in the dark.

Our mother and father were the ones who kept track of us. One parent or the other was always with us in those days, keeping the family bearings steady in the midst of all exterior distractions. My parents were both experienced navigators, after all. They had learned early on how to make their way from one place to the other, together and alone, anywhere in the world.

They had not always been so expert. My father himself marked that fact on his own record, when he wrote about flying to Mexico for the first time, and trying to find his way by doing what he had always done in the U.S.: flying low over the railroad stations to look for the name of each town as it appeared on the big sign above the station platform, then matching the name to one on the road maps he always carried with him. As far as the world below him was concerned then, an airplane was just a flying automobile, and a pilot could use the same geographical guides that a motorist did. There were no others, anyway. So my father flew low over the railroad stations of Mexico, and at the first one he found only one word, printed on a modest sign at one end of the station: "Caballeros." My father noted the word, ascended, and studied his maps, but could find no town called Caballeros. He concluded that this town must be too small to be on his road map, and flew on to another settlement. There he circled low over the railroad station again, and again found only one word on one sign: "Caballeros." It was not until the third or fourth town that my father began to suspect the truth: the meaning of the word "caballeros" in Spanish was "men's room."

Fortunately, despite such disorientations, my father managed to make his way to Mexico City, on that trip in 1928, and he met my mother there. Later, when they married, and flew together over many foreign countries in the early years of their marriage, my father was to make his wife not only his co-pilot, but his navigator as well. My mother, for most of her life, was a woman who did not lose her way. Not only that, but along with her instinctive good manners in any social situation, she was blessed with a gift for foreign languages.

In his whole life my father managed to learn only a few words of French, or German, or Italian, or Swahili, or whichever language he might feel he required in order to "get by," as he put it, in whatever country he was passing through. Again, he assumed that a grasp of general principles would be sufficient to his need. But quite often, according to the stories he told us with cheerful resignation on his return from those trips around the world, it turned out that the few words he had learned in a given language were not the ones he needed, after all. He remained completely undaunted by what others call "the language barrier," insisting that there was no such thing. Once when he could not communicate with words his wish for a boiled egg for a morning meal in Austria, he fell back on his knowledge of poultry, learned during his Minnesota farm days. He flapped his arms and clucked noisily at the astonished Gasthaus proprietor, in the manner of a self-satisfied laying leghorn.

"It worked," he told us proudly, and demonstrated his technique, in case any of the rest of us should ever find ourselves in a linguistic predicament at breakfast time.

More troubling, at least to our mother, was a story he told us about parking at the side of a busy street in Switzerland, very pleased after a long search to have found a free stretch of pavement to park in, just by the curb, right in the middle of town. As he got out of the car he waved at a charming little girl in braids, who was hopping up and down and calling loudly to him from the other side of the street.

"Die Strassenbahn! Die Strassenbahn!" the child shrieked. My father waved and smiled again, stretching his long legs comfortably after extracting himself from the driver's seat of the Volkswagen he drove around Europe in those days.

The little girl shrieked even louder, and gesticulated wildly.

"Die Strassenbahn!" Now she was pointing, as well as shrieking and hopping. My father turned in the direction she indicated and saw a streetcar (*Strassenbahn*), full of Swiss citizens at the end of their working day, heading his way. My father had parked at a streetcar stop. The conductor was bearing down upon him with the offended frown of Helvetian officialdom, and a heavy hand on the horn.

As children, on the grandmother trips, we spoke in no languages but our own, and had no particular interest in any but personal geography, either. We were content to sit together, after all the lights in the compartment had been extinguished by our father, looking out the window, naming names in the night. I don't know whether we identified the towns correctly. I know that Anne named the lights themselves, the long patterns of lights that lined the track before and after each station. We could see low flashes close by us, illuminating the rails, then much higher flashes above, as if on telephone poles, further away. At the same time we could hear the heavier rhythm of the train as it slowed on the way into the station, or picked up speed as it headed out of town.

The pattern of these lights became identified with the rhythm of the rails in my mind, and I can still feel the visual chant of the journeys west, if I close my eyes, can still see out the big window of the Pullman car, and can still hear my sister whispering the names she had invented for the lights of our night travel, first a high traveling name and then a low one, whispering these to herself and to us all, first slowly and far apart and then faster and closer together, like this: "plane light" (a high flash), "boat light" (a low one), plane light, boat light, plane light boat light, planelight boatlight planelightboatlight-planelightboatliiiii . . . Eventually her whisper was so fast that it was just a hiss, and the noise of the rails got smooth again because of the speed of the train traveling in open country. Soon the lights outside were gone entirely, and I was asleep, in the middle of the night, wedged in between the tight clean sheets of my Pullman bunk, heading halfway across the United States to Michigan.

12
Uncle

✳ T H E Detroit house of my Lindbergh grandmother
has become no more in my mind than a floating haze of sun-
light over bricks, outside, and a silence of empty rooms and
heavy furniture, within. In my memory it is not only a dark
but also a tall house, connected to a garden where once, on a
brick path, Scott used a magnifying glass to focus the sun's rays
and burn a hole in the rubber boot I was wearing, with my full
consent and intense interest. The smell of the burning rubber
is still with me, and the sight of the little round hole as it
slowly appeared, very small at first, like a hole made by a BB
gun (also familiar to me because of my brothers), and strangely
scorched-looking around the edges.

Inside the house, what little brightness there was came from
the pale blue eyes and the very white, wavy hair of our grandmother's brother, our great-uncle Charles Land. Evangeline, my
grandmother, had separated from my grandfather Lindbergh
while their son was still a toddler in Minnesota, though like
many estranged couples in those times, my father's parents
never divorced. Evangeline's brother came to live with her, as a
companion both for the mother and for her growing son, and
he remained in the household until Evangeline died in 1954.

Our names for this couple, sister and brother, make no

sense to me at all now. We called our grandmother "Farmor," which means "father's mother," in Swedish. But it was her estranged and long-dead husband, not Evangeline herself, who was Swedish. And as for our great-uncle, as far as I knew then, he had no name at all. We called him "Uncle," and we learned that our father and our grandmother had called him "Brother" when the three of them lived together. The families who knew him toward the end of his life, in Florida (where he paddled a canoe daily out into the Gulf of Mexico, off Fort Myers Beach, and once took Miss America for a ride), called him "Uncle John" for some reason. I never heard anyone call him by his real name, which was why for a long time I assumed he didn't have one. It seemed natural enough. He was a person whose existence was so clearly explained by his role in his family that any name had become irrelevant within it. He was "Brother," he was "Uncle," what other name could he need?

I learned his name when he came to live with us in Connecticut after his sister died, bringing hard, yellowish suitcases with thin, faded brown stripes around their middles, and "C.H. Land" in brown letters I could barely make out on top of the suitcases under the leather handles. His name was Charles, like my father's, and like my father's father's, too. But Uncle was from Evangeline's family, so his name was not Charles Lindbergh, like the others, but Charles Land, after his own father, the dentist from Detroit. I hope, thinking back, that the suitcases I saw were purchased for Uncle himself, and were not hand-me-downs from his father, but I suspect they may have been. The family was too thrifty, and Uncle too modest, for a suitcase monogrammed with his very own initials to have seemed a reasonable purchase, especially for a man who had lived for decades without even hearing his name.

It must have been confusing to have so many Charleses in the family, but I don't believe this was why Uncle went nameless. Most men named Charles acquire nicknames, after all: Chad, Chas, Chip, Chuck, Charlie . . . My Swedish grandfather was commonly known as "C.A." Lindbergh, and my father was called "Slim" by his military and aviation friends. Once in a while, too, I'd hear from somebody who had known my father as a boy, and claimed to have called him "Charlie." I found this so hard to believe that I wanted to ask, "And did he answer you?" My father was such a formal person, in his shy way. Though he was always courteous, and generally friendly, I could not imagine him ever being jocular enough to respond to "Charlie." If someone hailed him by that name when he walked by in the street, I thought he'd flinch, if he did anything, and keep on walking.

Uncle, for whatever reason, was always just "Uncle," a man of uncertain age and blue eyes, who held his body closely to himself, as if he were always cold, and wore his white hair combed back from his forehead in that smooth wave, a little longer than was the fashion in the 1950s. I liked Uncle's hairstyle. It made him look like pictures I had seen of the heroes of the old silent movies: Tom Mix, or Thomas S. Hart. For me, Uncle had all the romantic appeal of a bashful, handsome and lonely cowboy. I felt this way even though when I knew him, Uncle's life was not particularly romantic: he lived in Detroit, took care of his sister in her last illness, and made a small steam engine in her basement once, with real steam.

He made other things, too, that my brothers remember: miniature cannons and mortars, drawings, etchings on glass— Land told me about a picture Jon and Uncle made, delicate as lace, in a pane of glass in the double doors that led out of the house into the garden.

"It was a rat," Land said, "a really beautiful picture of a little rat. They made it with hydrofluoric acid, I don't know how. Uncle could make *anything*. I think that's basically what he did with his life. He took care of his sister, and he made things for Father while he was growing up. And later, when we came along, he took care of his sister, and he made things for us."

Scott remembers a target Uncle made, for shooting with .22 rifles. This also took place in the basement of the Detroit house, Scott says, and the target was another picture Uncle had drawn, not of a rat but a cat, or at least the rear view of a cat. It was drawn with all its hair on end and its back arched in fright. The bull's-eye was represented by a red-painted dot, placed exactly at the animal's anus.

"Father didn't like that cat one bit," Scott said, and I understood without further elaboration. Our father, who had an inclination toward practical jokery that we children thought hilarious, although our mother did not always agree—the short-sheeting of beds, the instigation of water fights, the elaborate pranks involving shaving cream or firecrackers—was visibly squeamish in the presence of what he considered vulgarity. Uncle, whom our father loved, at times embarrassed him deeply.

There were also some moments of head-shaking exasperation, after Uncle had come to live with us during the time following our grandmother's death. My father was especially concerned about the inventions: toothpaste that we were forbidden to try because of its possible toxicity, car polish that took the paint off the fender of one of the family cars when Uncle applied it, or so my father thought. In fact, Scott had taken the car out when he was not supposed to, and had scraped the fender in the usual way. Uncle, learning this, had loyally tried to account for the damage as best he could. When our father discovered it anyway, Uncle pretended that the whole thing was the fault of his own experimental chemistry.

Uncle's own car, which came with him from Detroit, though

it had been unused and up on blocks for years during his time there, was a 1941 Ford, exaggerated in height and volume, gleaming black and seeming as out-of-date to my eyes as a top hat, with some of the same elegance. I never saw and could not imagine him driving it—it was so large and expansive, he so thin and withdrawn, his only excesses the movie-star wave of his white hair, and the blue brightness of his eyes. Except, of course, for the dirty jokes, or "off-color stories" as they were referred to with embarrassment by the adult members of our Connecticut household. I did not understand them, but nonetheless knew that I was supposed to "overlook" Uncle's stories. My mother explained that these came from his youthful days in Canadian mining camps in the Great North Woods, a place where men were away from the company of women for many months at a time and had nothing better to do.

The basement at my grandmother's house in Detroit, where Uncle worked on his inventions, was darker even than the rest of the house. It was very dusty everywhere, too, with shelves full of what I now want to call "apothecary bottles"—murky vials that made you think of mad scientists and sorcerers, filled with obscure, certainly toxic, and probably explosive chemicals. All of his tools were there, too, and his workbench and a lathe. My brothers spent hours and even days in Uncle's workshop, on visits to our grandmother Lindbergh's house in the 1950s.

If they ever came out of the basement, Uncle and the boys could always go outside together into the garden and find snakes. The house was at the edge of the city, and snakes were plentiful in the area at that time. One day in Detroit Uncle and my brothers collected two galvanized-buckets-ful, and brought them all proudly into the house. But our grandmother, who was tolerant of many things, Land said, made them take all the snakes right back out again.

"Except one," he remembered. "One of them got away, and we just couldn't find it. It had kind of a funny-looking, stubby little tail, and it got loose somewhere in the house, I guess. It wasn't very big," he said, excusingly. I can hear in his voice my grandmother's indignation, and I try at the same time to hear her laughter. I know these were not the first boys in her household, and I cannot imagine, knowing my father, that they were the first snakes, either. Surely, sometime that day, she must have laughed.

This grandmother is a teasing mystery for me. My lack of knowledge about her is a hole in my understanding of the family. My father did not talk often about my grandmother Evangeline after her death, and I don't remember what he told me about her when she was living. What little I have learned about her is from his books, and from other people who knew her, but even that has been confusing and contradictory. Evangeline Lodge Land Lindbergh aroused strong emotions in people.

"Difficult," a Morrow aunt murmured.

"Neurotic," a cousin speculated.

"Crazy!" her stepdaughter Eva said to me, not long after my father's own death, with a vehemence that made me think she had only held her tongue for his sake. "I don't like to say it, but your grandmother was a crazy woman."

Eva told me stories that I have never heard from anyone else, of Evangeline inviting the ladies of Little Falls out from the town to visit the farm, then putting on a mocking, one-woman performance that cruelly satirized their provincial lifestyle. Eva said that Evangeline had once held a loaded pistol to my grandfather C.A.'s head as he sat at his desk. C.A. did not flinch, but told his wife wearily, as he sat very still in his office chair with the gun barrel pressed against his temple, that if this was what she had to do, she might as well go ahead and do it. At these words, Eva said, Evangeline flung the gun to the floor and ran off into the woods.

Eva told me that Evangeline had killed Eva's sister, Lillian, but she didn't tell me how. Lillian was my father's other half-sister. Like Eva, she was a daughter of C.A.'s first wife, Mary LaFond. I saw a portrait of Mary LaFond hanging in the farmhouse in Little Falls, a woman with a cloud of dark hair and a lovely, gentle face. In the portrait she has a little smile on her lips, expressing private amusement overlaid with kindness. She looks as if one of her children has just said something endearing and ridiculous, but she does not want to cause embarrassment by laughing. She looks like a mother any child would miss with all of its heart, for all of the rest of the child's life.

My impression was that of the two girls, Lillian lacked her sister, Eva's, strength of body and will, and that the family instinctively protected her greater vulnerability. Lillian died in 1916, at the age of twenty-nine, of tuberculosis. By then she was married and a mother, living in California. I know that my father and his mother drove across the country from the farm in Little Falls, in a memorably temperamental early car they called "Maria," to visit the young couple one summer. How had Evangeline "killed" Lillian though? What did Eva mean?

There was much revealed, but much more left unsaid, in the conversations I had with my father's sister, during the brief time I knew her as an adult. Eva had visited us once or twice in Connecticut when we were growing up, but we were not closely connected with the Minnesota family, possibly because my father knew how his half-sister felt about Evangeline. When he spoke about Eva herself it was with affection and enthusiasm. She had courage, character, and "grit," he said. She was one of a kind. Eva in turn spoke of my father, after he died, as an energetic toddler, "full of the dickens," and chuckled at the memory. I was startled and pleased. I had never before met anyone who knew my father this way.

But after my father's death Eva walked through the old farmhouse at Little Falls with me, now part of the Lindbergh Home and Historical Site, and heard a guide describe the painting on one or two delicate china pieces as Evangeline's own handwork. She became indignant.

"She never painted those," Eva said to me in a disgusted whisper. "She wasn't capable of it."

Eva was then in her mid-eighties, tall and thin and adamant, with a strong spirit and a keen eye. At fourteen, she told me, she finally ran away from home, and from her stepmother (in whose care she had been left by C.A. at the time he separated from Evangeline). When Eva's father learned of her defection all he said, Eva told me, was "I couldn't live with her, and you don't have to, either."

Eva, ten years older than my father, was a woman to be reckoned with all her life. In her later teens Eva clambered out the windows of Carleton College, in the night, to attend a cookout on the river. She was first married to George Christie, and raised two children, then was widowed and married again, to Howard Spaeth. She kept all of the names for her lifetime. Considering that she had earned them, she just added each one as it came along, and called herself Eva Lindbergh Christie Spaeth. In their later years she and her husband Howard once were robbed by youthful burglars, whom Eva lectured energetically until they left the house.

"You're a strong, good-looking boy, and you should be doing something better with your life than stealing," Eva told one intruder. "And don't tell me it's because you're 'hungry.' If you're hungry, go to the kitchen and get yourself some food."

My mother felt both wary of her mother-in-law and sorry

for her, I think. Her published letters to her husband's mother are open and affectionate, but I remember that whenever "Mrs. Lindbergh's" name came up in conversation, there was a flutter of excusings, and a sense of ruffled feathers to be smoothed, misunderstandings to be cleared up, topics to be avoided in conversation. My mother once suggested to me that "Farmor" and "Uncle" were products of a marriage in which the parents were so devoted to one another that the children felt left out of the circle of affection. My mother also guessed that my Lindbergh grandmother went west from Detroit as an idealistic young schoolteacher from the city, lured by unrealistic ideas about the romance of the frontier. Evangeline was not at all prepared for small-town life in Minnesota, my mother speculated, or for marriage to an older man, a handsome widower with two young girls to raise, a dour husband who expected his young wife to do the child-rearing, among her other responsibilities and obligations.

"I think," my mother once said to me in an enlightened way, as if she had just thought of it, "that your grandmother was afraid of sex."

I can only remember Evangeline Lindbergh firsthand, myself, as a face in a bed, a portrait framed by her own bedsheets, her features no more than a pale smoothness over bones. I did not tell my father, at the time of our visits to her house, how uneasy she made me, this grandmother who was just a covered-up heap and shape of stillness. And I never told him years later, in the mid-1960s, when I saw in an annotated, illustrated edition of the play *Marat/Sade* a reproduction of the etching called *The Death Mask of Marat*, that I recognized in it, not the French revolutionary, but my Detroit grandmother in her bed.

Her bed was in the living room, a common enough situation in long illnesses, but one that was new to me at my age. The oddness of it became for me a further deepening of the dim, unfathomable quality of that house: a bed with a shape in it, lamps, a bookcase, a sofa, all of them in shadow. And yet the one thing I can see clearly in my memory of that scene is my grandmother's smile. She smiled at my father, from her bed, with lingering tenderness. The look that passed between those two was so loving that even I could feel the nature of it, and was calmed. I was afraid of her stillness, and I didn't like her pale mouth and cheek—if I had been asked to kiss her, I would have run from the room—but I was held there, and soothed in spite of myself, by the smile. It is the only time I can remember seeing any expression on her face at all.

She tried to say something. She could not speak well enough for me to understand what it was, the sound of her voice was so wet and weak, the words so slurred together. But my father understood her meaning, or pretended to—I'm still not sure which. He told us that our grandmother wanted to offer us "malted milk" tablets, which had been a favorite treat of my father's in his own childhood, and may have been considered a tonic of some kind, too, a healthy dose of malt to strengthen youthful constitutions. These tablets were kept in another dusty-looking medicine bottle, on the highboy near where she lay, and as soon as I saw the bottle I did not want to have anything to do with whatever came out of it. Furthermore, when shaken out into my father's palm as carefully as if they were so many gold nuggets, the tablets themselves looked as uninviting and out-of-date to my eyes as giant, moldering aspirin pills. How was I going to swallow such a thing?

I tried to be obedient and respectful, as befitted the era and my upbringing. I made a vow to myself, too, that no matter how terrible the next few seconds might be, I would not choke or vomit. Thus stoically prepared, I selected one of the clay-colored capsules, thrust it quickly back toward my molars, and bit down into one of the great surprises of my life. Malted milk tablets were delicious. The taste that touched my tongue and spread everywhere through my mouth was as rich and deep and delightful as chocolate, which I adored. I was mesmerized, astonished, completely seduced. I chewed, sucked, and drizzled malted milk into the greedy moistness of my inner cheeks while I stared at my father and my grandmother, and I felt an unsuspected melting pleasure of belonging draw itself gently over me. It had been there all the time, without my noticing it, like an old family eiderdown that might have been folded at the foot of my grandmother's bed, certainly by now as full of dust as of feathers. Yet it was still ample enough, and still warm enough, to cover and comfort every person in the darkened house.

Looking back at that room and that moment, I try to put myself in my father's place. What was he thinking, this tall man who sat in darkness between his dying mother and his twitchy, reluctant child, with his hand held out in offering? My father's cupped palm was very unlike the back of his hand, to begin with. He had an outdoorsman's fist, as knuckled and gnarled as mountains and trees, its veins running close to the surface like streams iced over, pale blue between freckles with a few interesting hairs. His grasp was strong. It would tighten on crisp days over ax-handles, kerosene cans, and armloads of firewood that came into our house through the doors with gusts of autumn wind smelling of sharp scents of pine and fire. But his palm was different: smooth, with the smell of pencil shavings and carbon paper, and it was as shiny in its rounded places as the inside of a shell. It was from that palm, in some studied and angular priesthood, that my father administered communion to the three generations of his family that day in Detroit, with malted milk tablets.

13
Alone in
Her Trouble

✳ I THINK about malted milk tablets today and wonder whether they would help me to make a link, as my father once did, between my own mother's old age, and my own child's uncomprehending youth. I feel the hopelessness of this task every time I try to explain to my young son what has happened to his grandmother as a result of her age and a series of strokes. I wish he could understand why she sometimes behaves as she does these days. I wish he could understand what she is, or was, "really like." And yet, at the same time, I am beginning to realize that such an understanding cannot be forced, and that it is a false one, anyway. For him, the fact is that his grandmother is "really like" what she is really like now, as he knows her.

Benjamin was four years old when my mother was first hospitalized for a stroke, in 1991. Because he does not remember her from before that time, he will remember her as she is now. She, on her side, cannot truly know this clowning, talkative grandson, who uses big words in conversation whether or not he can pronounce or fully understand them, who reads a lot, writes out long adventure stories in notebooks or on the computer, and tells riddles, from bad to worse, until the family begs for mercy.

How my mother would have enjoyed his wordplay, even at its most awful, and how he would have delighted in her enjoyment at another time in their lives. How often, knowing this, I have tugged and tugged, trying to force them together like a jacket that won't fit. I can't stop wanting them to be more to one another than a mere overlapping in time.

"She's not really like this," I pleaded with Ben one spring afternoon, when his grandmother was in a particularly agitated state. "She's had strokes—you know, we've talked about what strokes are, and how they can affect people. Her brain isn't working right. It isn't her fault."

"I don't care!" he replied, white-faced and furious with the righteous anger that follows fear. "I hate her! I don't care what anybody says. You can love her if you want, but I hate her!"

My mother, in the grip of her own irrational fears, had stolen Ben's ice cream. She had swooped down upon him at our own dinner table and had snatched his dessert away just as he was about to take his first bite. Trembling with illogical certainty, unshakable in confusion, she insisted that this ice cream was "poisoned," and she began to move with the bowl toward the kitchen sink, intent on dumping the contents there. When I tried to halt her progress ("No! It's okay, Mother. This is *good* ice cream.") she slapped at my hands, her little body tense, her face as tight with fury as my son's.

I had read a good deal about "disorientation" and "confusion" and "dementia" in old people, during the months when my mother's first post-stroke symptoms began to appear. I was aware that, along with fear of theft, fear of poisoning was a common theme. I also knew that this batch of Ben & Jerry's Cherry Garcia was not poisoned. At the very same time, I could sympathize with my mother's anger. She was trying to save her grandson from a life-threatening emergency, while I, his own mother, was attempting to stop her—what an outrage! Of course she hated my interference, just as much as Ben hated hers.

He sat, embarrassed and horrified in his chair, watching his grandmother and his mother struggle over his bowl, witnessing both my fretful anxiety and the flutter of little slaps my mother gave me when I took the plate away. He saw her two open hands beating at my wrist, their movement like the panicked flappings of a captive bird against my arm. Each separately justified, each differently isolated in time, my mother and my son were both passionate, and I could not think of a way to comfort either one of them, let alone myself, that day.

Now, years later, that period of my mother's intense agitation and anger is far behind us. She and Ben and I sat together peacefully just the other day, while she and I drank tea in front of her fireplace in her home in Vermont in early October, and he built a Swiss village on the rug. He was using wooden pieces that had come from her house in Switzerland in a net bag, none of the figures more than two inches high: wooden houses with sharp-pitched red roofs, a group of wooden fences in sections, a wooden cow and horse, six human shapes in different colors, featureless and barely more than two-dimensional in their jigsaw outlines.

"This is the village," said Ben as we watched him and sipped our tea, my mother calmly silent while the houses were placed next to one another, one, two, and three, cheek to jowl under their peaked red tops like a trio of red-capped gnomes. In front of them he arranged the fences in a square, and put the horse and cow inside their boundaries.

"This is the barnyard," he said. I nodded. It looked right to me. Beyond the fence, a little way from the houses, two of the human figures were placed, as if outside the village, in conversation.

"Those are your helpers," Ben said, flashing a quick look at his grandmother, who looked back at him, poker-faced. "They're taking a walk." My mother's caregiver smiled from her chair near the fire.

There were four human figures left. He put them between the houses and the barnyard, all together.

"This is the family," he said. One of the figures was purple, one red, one yellow. My mother was wearing a purple velour turtleneck and matching pants, one of a series of similar outfits she wears regularly, comfortable but elegant-looking cousins to the sweatsuits I see joggers wearing in cold weather, with pins or scarves to dress them up if she's in the mood.

Ben looked at her, then at the purple wooden figure.

"This is the grandmother," he said, picking it up and holding it out for her to see, with his shyest smile. He looked quickly at his grandmother, making eye contact, and then quickly away, just in case.

"Good," she said to him, nothing else. He went on playing, she went on watching, and I finished my tea, and warmed myself by the fire. Relationships are rarely perfect, whether between individuals or between generations, but a little warmth can go a long way.

Even at its most extreme, including the week of Ben's stolen ice cream, my mother's wild period was relatively brief. In the five years since the first strokes and the resulting memory loss began to affect her behavior, there has been only one month when she seemed actively out of control: throwing food, breaking things, tearing up letters, books, and photographs and throwing them in the fire or flushing them down the toilet, slapping or shoving people. Her physical activity at that time, the whirlwind energy propelled by the anger, made a strong impression upon those of us who witnessed it, but in fact it did not cause much real damage. My mother is a small woman, who has had little experience with violent behavior. To be perfectly frank, she was not very good at it.

This particular wildness possessed her most completely just a few months after Anne's death. I think now that it may have been a way of expressing her grief at the loss of her daughter, mixed with a frustrated anguish over her own survival at such an age and in such a condition. It eases my mind to believe this, but I have other reasons for believing it, too.

"They must have mixed up the names," she said to me, when I told her, at the beginning of December in 1993, that my sister, Anne, was dying. At the time I took her response to the terrible news as a further sign of her confusion, and some self-preserving form of what is popularly called "denial." I was relieved, because I thought that to see my mother's direct, full-blown grief over Anne would have been too much for me to bear, on top of my own feelings. And yet, my mother's agitation, when it reached its height a few months after my sister's death, was itself more than I could bear. Guilt-ridden and ashamed—had I not moved her from her home in Connecticut purposely after Anne's death, so that neither she nor I would be alone with this loss?—I retreated from my mother in every way I could think of, for a while.

She was living just a hundred yards up the road from my home that year, in the house modeled after the one in Switzerland. There were trained caregivers with her at all times, as there have been since her hospitalization. Although my mother is fortunate in being financially able to live at home rather than in a nursing care facility, her physical and mental states are both so unsteady that she cannot be alone, and she needs a degree of care that family members cannot provide. At that time she could no longer manage dressing, washing, or going to the bathroom by herself. She had little sense of day or night, and was often overcome by terrors and urgencies that made her want to flee from wherever she was. In Vermont, she might try to run down the road in midwinter at midnight, in her nightgown. In Connecticut, she might break away from her caregivers and rush into a store, accosting a stranger with her fears—that she was being held captive, that she was being poisoned, that people were "after her." She might be afraid of her food, or of the people around her, or of her medicine. One day she refused to take even her low-dose blood-pressure pills, on another day she tried to take all of her medicines at once, believing this would save her life. The sedatives and calming drugs prescribed by doctors for this kind of agitated confusion helped her sometimes, but not always.

Even with the advantage of wealth, even surrounded by family, even with the kindest and most constant of care, my mother seemed, above all, so alone in her trouble. She seemed so little, so delicate, so desperate. We all responded—family members, caregivers, physicians, and friends alike—as if to the plight of a beautiful, cruelly neglected child. Everything she did, everything she said, we regarded as urgent, compelling, heartbreaking, and true, even when we knew it wasn't. It was impossible not to believe her.

"Tie me to the mast!" my sister whispered to me one beautiful fall day in 1991, like Ulysses tempted by Sirens. It was six months after the strokes, and our mother begged and contradicted herself fervently, over and over, on a drive home to Connecticut following a two-day visit to Vermont. She was changing her mind roughly once every hour about whether we should be taking her north or south.

"Take me home to Darien! Please!" she cried plaintively in White River Junction, toward the beginning of the trip. We assured her that we were doing just that.

"I want to go back to Vermont!" she told us in Greenfield,

Massachusetts, after two more hours of driving. And so it went, all the way down the highway, first "I want to go back!" and then "I want to go home!"

She had been so eager to get away from her home in Darien that week that Anne and I had driven the six hours it took us to get there, picked her up, and turned right around again to bring her north to Vermont. We drove together because there had been a few times recently when our mother had tried to get out of a moving automobile, and it was not safe to drive with her if there was only one person in the car. She was content on the drive north this time, but she lasted only twenty-four hours in her house here before the fears took over, and she wanted to "go home."

Anne and I both had children in school, and work to do, but it was clear that our own schedules would have to yield to our mother's trouble. It was going to consume us one way or the other, in any case. So we got in the car again and tried once more to carry out her wishes.

It was so hard to keep pace with her demands! And yet at some profound level of understanding, her contradictory appeals rang true to us every time she made them. The desperation, if nothing else, was as undeniable as it was heartrending.

After Anne died, though, I lost my way. For the first time in my life I could not understand or respond to my mother's emotions at all. I was alone with too much loss, and I was being carried along too fast in a stream of experiences that were new to me. I was afraid, with a fear too sharp and perilous to accommodate empathy. I went numb.

"I'm dying. Why won't you call the doctor?" My mother would greet me at her door in Vermont with these words every day, stopping only to utter them before she returned to pacing back and forth between her bedroom and the living room sofa. Her caregivers reported she had been doing this for most of the day. She was unable to rest either on her bed or on the sofa for longer than a few minutes at a time, before getting up and moving again, back and forth, along the same path.

"I'm dying. Call the doctor."

It made no difference that we had, in fact, called the doctor, minutes before. It made no difference even if she had seen the doctor that very morning. If she were reminded of such day-time truths, her face would close like a trapdoor in refusal.

"I don't believe you." And the walking would continue, with the refrain.

"I'm dying. Call the doctor. Why won't you call the doctor?" The note of reproach, the face of accusation, the pacing. Thirty, forty, fifty, a hundred times in an hour, back and forth. It must have been a kind of torture for her, a hellish, endless repetition. She was perpetually dying; I, her daughter, perpetually and heartlessly watching her die, and the doctor was never sum-moned.

From my perspective, weighed down by loss and by the accumulated exhaustion of the previous year, it was hellish, too. I could not feel sympathy, only irritation. *My mother does nothing but complain!* I mentally muttered as I watched her moving across the room. *Not only that, but she only cares about herself! Why doesn't she ever mention Anne?* Anne's dying had been *real*, not this unfounded, self-centered melodrama. I, who had sat vigil with my sister for month after month, could not sit for even half an hour with my mother in this state.

But it had been so easy to be with Anne. I, along with the many others who loved her and spent time with her while she was sick—her husband, her two children, her friends—did so as much for myself as for my sister. It was Anne herself, all through the chemotherapy and the many kinds of surgery, through the surges of hope and the terrible disappointments, who kept all the rest of us going, every day, for a year and a half.

Anne had a way of encapsulating reality, making each piece of it that she had elected to consider—the rain, the birds at the window, a swim in the river, wet leaves on the grass—much more important than the hovering inevitability of her own illness. Each morsel of time spent with us was fully real-ized. She didn't dwell on some other time. We played cards on her bed in the chemotherapy ward, and she beat me at black-jack many times. ("Loser buys coffee—Sorry, Reeve, but it *had* to be you. I'm a little tied up here.") She sat reading after surgery, her son's baseball cap jammed tight on her head back-ward, as he had taught her, to hold steady the tubes that went from her nose into her stomach so that they could not pull at her throat. She came out of her last operation on Halloween on a hospital gurney, rolling her eyes at us as the six-foot male attendant rolled her body back into her room. The attendant had chosen to observe the holiday in a wig, a woman's black dress, stockings, and high heels. Anne's own feet in hand-knit wool socks ("I find I get cold feet *after* the operation, not before") stuck out from under the white sheet that covered the rest of her like twin semaphores, signaling with green stripes and pink hearts that she herself had knitted into them her way of living: *Stay warm . . . Keep laughing . . . I love you, no matter what the circumstances . . . and no matter what the circumstances, don't take yourself too seriously . . .*

She died two weeks before Christmas, and her daughter gave me, for Christmas, a pair of Anne's hand-knit wool socks. I wore them wherever I went, but even wearing them, there were days when I could not walk to our mother's house at all.

On other days I could face her quite boldly, walking up to the house as if for a casual visit, in spite of my fear. But then, if "anything happened," I would beat a hasty retreat. I was like Ben, who had very reluctantly agreed, some days after the ice cream incident, to go back up the hill to his grandmother's house for dinner.

"But if she does *one* weird thing," he warned, "I'm out of there!"

And so was I. I walked back to my own house from my mother's one afternoon with my shirt dripping V8 juice and my mind boiling insult and outrage. My mother had been offered a glass of V8 by a gentle caregiver during my visit, and instead of drinking it she had thrown it, glass and all, catching me full on the breast of a blouse I had picked up from the dry-cleaner's that very day. I turned and left the house, and as I walked home down the road I watched the red juice drip onto the gravel and dirt, and said to myself through clenched teeth, "This is my heart's blood, and *I* am dying."

I too have a taste for melodrama, but there is something in my character that lacks the stamina to sustain it. Long before I reached my door, I was telling myself, "No, it isn't, and no, you're not. This is V8 juice, on a clean shirt, and you're furious. Period."

I try to think that my mother's action was some expression of emotion in response to Anne's death, perhaps a raging impulse to die in her daughter's place. At least I can forget the V8 juice, if I believe this, and the thought brings me peace because it honors both of them, both of my Annes, whom I miss so much.

I think that the relationships of my mother's life are with her now only in a general way, in a kind of mingling. It doesn't really matter which of us is which. Her children, her grandchildren, her parents and her siblings, her sons and daughters, and herself—all are interchangeable. It is as if she has released us from the specific details of relationships, and kept the overall benevolence, which she feathers out over the whole bunch of us, warm and indiscriminate, like a broody hen.

Sometimes, however, this can be disconcerting.

"I have a letter here about Con's death," she said to me one May, as we sat together on the sofa in her living room in Connecticut. Her sister Constance Morrow Morgan, our "Aunt Con," had died at the end of March 1995 in Portland, Oregon. Before I could respond, though, my mother turned her head to look at me with patient curiosity, and queried, "But aren't you Con?"

"Sometimes," I wanted to say, because it seemed to me to be by far the most truthful answer, but I could not say it. For my mother it may have been true, but in me it was lunacy. I explained instead that I was her daughter Reeve. Her sister Con had died in March. We had been sending flowers to the hospital and to the house all during Con's illness, and Con knew that my mother had sent them. I said that we had also telephoned many times to inquire about Con, and had learned that she kept a picture of my mother on her bureau, and that she loved to look at it from her bed. I went on at some length about the circumstances of Con's illness and death, as gently as possible, but my mother had stopped listening long before I stopped talking, and had picked up a magazine on the table in front of her. I was, not for the first time, left babbling in midair.

I find myself doing this often, verbally treading water or dog-paddling my brain around in some felt reservoir of what is real, factual, actually *here*. I am trying hard to keep afloat and anchored in time and place, as I have to do, while other people move away or move on, as they must. The end of connection, the end of relationship, is such a dissolving phenomenon that it is very difficult to maintain balance. Little by little, quickly or slowly, the ties unbind, however we may continue to cling to each and every shred that has held loved ones together, one to the other, for so many years.

I think back and wonder what my father saw in his mother's loving smile in the midst of her stillness. I wonder if she smiled often, and if she did, was that enough for him to hang his old affection on, and keep it steady and unwavering through her illness, even to the time of her death? A smile does help, I know, to keep the current flowing when words are disappearing and conversation is minimal. Absence of expression on a beloved face translates so easily into absence of feeling, in the mind of the beholder. If I am with my mother for an hour or so without our exchanging a word, I can still savor our silence together. Silence has always been a rich medium and mood for the two of us. But if I am with her for a long period, for a week, say, when there is little or no change of expression on her face, I feel bereft of our relationship. I lose my old, deep sense of our attachment, and with it some of my bearings in this life. It is at times truly catastrophic to me that I can no longer find myself reflected, as if in a mirror, in my own mother's face.

Lately I have rediscovered her hands. In self-defense, I look down at them from the blankness of her face, and I know, with a welcome surge of affection, that they at least have not changed. If I take one of her hands in one of my own hands, she does not seem to mind, even in her most distant moments. I like to feel the shape and the warmth of her hand, and I am reassured by it. I have known this hand, my mother's hand, all my life, and it has known me, too. It knows me still. I can tell that this is true, whatever her face may show or not about our connection. If I just sit quietly and hold my mother's hand these days, whether or not I understand my family's losses, I can at least take heart in what remains.

Three days before she died, my sister threatened to kill me. I don't know why. She was full of morphine and made no sense when she talked. All those around her tried to be attentive and comforting and not too obvious in our suspended state, waiting for her death. I could not believe, even as I waited, that she would die, but I could not believe that she would live, either. Uncomfortable, sitting with and without her, I tried to make a joke—something about the hospital bed, the commode, the tubes and wires—usually I could make her laugh, using as she did a reference point in her immediate surroundings. Making Anne laugh, entertaining her, had always been my job.

This time she did not laugh. Instead she rose from the bed and came after me, her hair slicked back against her skull, her bones sharp, her eyes hollow, her gown flapping. She did not look at all like my sister, my Ansy, she looked like a banshee, gaunt and threatening, and she staggered toward me unsteadily, saying, "I'm going to kill you, Reeve!"

Her arms were outstretched in front of her like a sleepwalker's, with the palms up, and her tongue was stuck out as far as it could go, pointing with a child's unmitigated malevolence straight at me. I was terrified.

I retreated backward through the room, the big living room in the house in Thetford, Vermont, where she had come home from the hospital after the doctors had said there was nothing else they could do for her. I had two things in my mind as I stumbled backward, she stumbling after me. The first was a bargaining chant from the depth of my stunned memory, the bottom of the barrel of my long-ago embattled Little Sister mind: *What did I do to you? What do you want from me? I'll give you anything—my dolls, my tricycle, all my stuffed animals— anything; just stop making that face!*

The second thought was that I knew my sister's tongue, protruding and pointed at me, better than my own. It was a part of my family, I had known it forever, and it would never be anything but familiar to me. Anne could touch it to the tip of her nose, making me jealous because my own broad fat tongue would not extend that far out of my own mouth, Anne could stick it in my face, as she was doing now, and contort it to threaten me in any evil way she wanted to. But whatever she did, I was safe, because I knew that tongue, her tongue, and because I knew it, I knew it could not hurt me.

I walked backward and fixed my attention on my sister's tongue, not her words, not her face, not her wild eyes, only her tongue, as if on the one hope of salvation in a desperate world. But then I saw out of the corner of my eye an impatient look cross Anne's face, and she stretched her arms farther out in my direction, and stumbled again. The nurse at her elbow moved in closer, but at once I understood the moment in a different way. I put out my own hands toward my sister, who took them, and in taking them, steadied herself.

There was no change of expression or purpose—her tongue was still out, her body still coming toward me, though her energy was almost completely sapped. We only walked together for a few yards, in all, before she collapsed onto a sofa. But I had seen and known the powerful familiarity of her tongue, and I had reached out and held her two unsteady, homicidal older sister's hands, and I had therefore made it possible for her to come and kill me, whatever that meant, and this was enough for both of us. Together, tightly holding each other's hands, one of us beyond reason and the other beyond fear, we two sisters were thus able to move, I backward and she forward, over the threshold and into the next room.

14

Morrows and Maine

✳ I F my father's mother, Farmor, was the grandmother of mystery, then my mother's mother, known as
Grandma Bee, was the grandmother of manners and tradition. At her houses, and there were three of them—
one in New Jersey, one in Mexico, and one in Maine—
grandchildren dressed well and ate "nicely," among finger
bowls and monogrammed napkins, molded butter balls
and silver tea services, fine porcelain and beloved family
antiques, under the intelligent amused gaze of Elizabeth
Cutter Morrow.

I never saw my Morrow grandmother lying down. I
remember this in sharp contrast to my Undbergh grandmother, who in her illness and dependency I never saw
standing up. I don't know how tall Farmor was, or what
her physical attitudes and gestures were, because I don't
have a full-sized, mobile memory to draw upon, only that
still tableau in the dark living room: the single smile, the
pale face and paler bedclothes, the gentle attentiveness of
her son, my father. In the room where she lay I could sense
in a vague vaporous way remnants of past activity and past
emotion, like the clinging indefinite scents of meals served
long ago. But the atmosphere in the Detroit house was so
distantly flavored by these: passion, tension, the visitations
of fear or neurosis, tenderness, humor, action, restraint, all

were calm and far away, all quieted in darkness. By the time I knew her there was nothing about my father's mother, neither flesh nor spirit, that was still visibly in motion.

Grandma Bee, on the other hand, really got around. I assume that she did not move as quickly in my day as she had in earlier years. I can remember seeing a walking stick in her hand once, and a whole intriguing bouquet of them in the umbrella stand by the front door of the house in Maine. These were made of highly polished wood, walnut or ash, and most of them were curled over at the top in the traditional manner. One was silver-handled, with the dark elegance of ebony down the stem. Another was gnarled and knobby in spirals, like a twisty little wind-blown gnome. The canes did not figure in my mind as a sign of weakness in my grandmother. To me they were just another decorative element in her atmosphere, a merely playful option, like the croquet set on the lawn.

My grandmother Morrow played croquet and gardened and went to church and golfed with equal energy. Everything she did had a cheerful intensity of purpose about it, whether she was sending an opponent's croquet ball off into the woods, or singing a hymn at the Presbyterian church on Sundays—*"Dear Lord and Father of mankind, forgive our foolish ways."* It was inconceivable that the Lord to whom she lifted her voice, surely a Father with plenty of good humor and common sense— would *not* forgive my grandmother's foolish ways—if she had any. She must have been so useful to Him as an instrument of harmony and order.

Even when she sat down, Grandma Bee sat with intent: presiding at dinners and at tea times, entertaining children and visitors, playing cards, writing notes on white or blue squares of notepaper with matching envelopes that had "Deacon Brown's Point," the name for the property in Maine, or "Next

Day Hill," the name for the New Jersey house, printed neatly at the top, and often, with all of us gathered around the armchair in her room, reading aloud to her grandchildren.

Grandma Bee wrote several children's books of her own, including two with illustrations by a friend, artist René D'Harnoncourt. One of these was called *The Painted Pig*, a story about two Mexican children and a piggy bank. Another, *Beast, Bird, and Fish*, was an alphabetical songbook published by Alfred A. Knopf in 1933. Along with the verses and the paintings this book included music, written by Eberhard D'Harnoncourt. I take a copy of this book with me to read to children today when I am invited to a school as a visiting author. Although language in children's books of 1933 tended to be more formal than it is now, my grandmother's verses, read aloud, still appeal strongly to children.

B

A Bear is white or black or brown
And likes some ice to sit upon
He has an overpowering hug
And when he dies, becomes a rug

T

A Turtle carries her home on her head
And draws in her feet when she goes to bed.
She pulls down the roof to shut out the light
And never brushes her teeth at night!

My father's favorite verse from *Beast, Bird, and Fish* was a short one that accompanied the letter E, for Elephant. He would recite it while carrying me around the Darien house on his shoulders:

"The elephant should never sneeze
It shakes the ground and all the trees"

Six feet two inches tall, balding on top and thick-chested in the middle, my father rocked back and forth in heavy-footed rhythm as I clung to his neck and shrieked with delight, *"DON'T, FATHER! HELP! YIKES!"* Ignoring my screams, though occasionally removing my clasping hands from his windpipe and replacing them on his shoulders, he would walk along and repeat the rhyme in a slow, monotonous chant that put emphasis on every other syllable, to match his elephantine, left-foot, right-foot pace:

"The EL-e-PHANT should NEVer SNEEZE,
It SHAKES the GROUND, and ALL the TREES!"

At the end, he gave an elephant-sized sneeze that shook his whole body, and dumped me onto a nearby sofa. Disheveled and laughing, my father would then take the slim black Ace comb out of his trouser pocket, and comb one gray-white lock of hair, the one that he allowed to grow long for this purpose and which I was allowed, on special and very brief occasions, to braid into a skinny gray pigtail that hung lopsidedly over his ear, carefully back over the bald spot on the top of his head, and across to the other side. After that he would disappear into his office and type away with two fingers, very fast, for hours.

I have an old affection for *Beast, Bird, and Fish,* and a new respect, because I, too, have written a rhyming alphabet book for children, and I know how hard it is to come up with, for instance, a rhyme starting with the letter X, unless the writer chooses to take the same tired old "X-ray" and "Xylophone" route that so many alphabet book authors have traveled. My own solution was to cheat and use the word "eXpelled" (in *The*

Awful Aardvarks Go to School). My grandmother, more inge-
nious, wrote this on the X page:

> Xantolumpus:
> *I found him in the dictionary*
> *(I think he looks a little scary)*

D'Harnoncourt's pictures of Xantolumpus are varied and mon-
strous, but when I first looked this creature up in the dictio-
nary, I couldn't find him anywhere, and learned to my delight
that he was a joke.

My grandmother wrote longer stories as well, describing her
own children and the life of her growing family: *The Rabbit's
Nest, A Pint of Judgment,* and *Shannon,* a tribute to a beloved
family dog. These books, like the picture books done with the
D'Harnoncourts, were written with perception and humor, but
when I read them I am sharply aware that my grandmother
wrote, and my mother grew up, in a very different part of the
century than I did. In the young Morrow family, children made
"penwipers" for their fathers, and hemmed lace handkerchiefs
for their mothers for Christmas. In my grandmother's books
the mothers and grandmothers wore floor-length dresses every
day, with puffed shoulders and tiny waists like Gibson Girls,
while the uncles, in dark suits and Theodore Roosevelt mus-
taches, slapped their knees when amused, and used expressions like "perfectly swell."

In the informal, postwar years of my own childhood, it was
a joy to have Grandma Bee read to us from any book, of any
era. The older cousins remember Kipling, and Enid Blyton,
and old issues of *St. Nicholas* magazine. I remember furniture
and atmosphere more than books: an upholstered armchair, a
reading lamp, and the gathered comfort of a small, warm room
at night. I remember hearing the story of *Babar,* by Jean de

Brunhoff, and that I hated the beginning part, where the elephant mother gets shot in the jungle, just as I hated the equivalent episode in Felix Salten's *Bambi*. Why did these authors have to kill off the mothers early on in their stories, leaving children with watery eyes and lumps in their throats for the rest of the book? But then there were the thrilling, rags-to-riches adventures of the young elephants, Babar and Arthur and Celeste, who began their lives in the heart of the jungle and became royal elephants, dressed in golden crowns and business suits. And who could resist the wiry energy and cleverness of the monkey Zephyr, an earlier, less outrageous Curious George?

I was especially attracted to Babar's human patroness, the wise, thin, rich old lady in a clinging black dress. Though she was not herself an elephant, the old lady understood elephants, and supported the elephant community in every possible way. My grandmother Morrow's benevolence toward grandchildren —croquet matches, new bicycles at Christmas time, trips to Mexico and to Maine—was very much like the old lady's kindness to elephants, although the two ladies dressed differently, and were not at all the same shape.

My grandmother Morrow was a woman of small but sturdy stature, with remarkably tiny feet. Her daughters were not much bigger, feet included. My mother achieved a ladies size 5 shoe in adulthood, but Grandma Bee never took anything bigger than a 3 or a 4. As for Aunt Con, I remember that in an upstairs closet of her own house in Maine, when I was a teenager, there was a box of summer shoes of all shapes and sizes, labeled generously, "If the shoe fits . . ." I remember, too, finding out that if the shoe was Aunt Con's, it never did.

My sister and I, with normal shoe sizes for our age and era, felt that we represented a generation of large-footed louts. Our father offered us some consolation. His shoe size was double the size of our mother's, and larger than any of his sons'. Moreover, much as he respected the Morrows, he believed that bigger (i.e., Lindbergh) feet were healthier feet. He encouraged his children to go without shoes in summer, for the full extension and proper development of our toes. For winter wear, he ordered for us each year from a company called Totem-Moc, long before L.L. Bean had come into our lives, two pairs of leather moccasins, one with soles for daily use, and one without, to serve as slippers. He trimmed their dangling leather laces with his penknife, then double-square-knotted them and glued the knots closed for all eternity with Duco Cement. Duco Cement was his glue of choice, as Ford and Volkswagen were his automobiles and Ammodent his tooth powder, during those years. I inhaled the fumes deeply and happily as he applied gooey thicknesses of the stuff to my properly shod foot, preserving me from the clumsiness of my loose-laced peers. Later in life, when I learned that glue sniffing was addictive, I could understand why. I still enjoy the smell of wet glue, though I gave up the moccasins for three-inch heels in high school. In direct defiance of my father's philosophy and teachings, I tottered along on these for a few years, until the 1960s. Then, like so many others, I was barefoot, sandaled, or even moccasined once again.

Despite her diminutive size, my grandmother had a large moral presence. A scholar, an educator, an elder of the First Presbyterian Church of Englewood, New Jersey, for a time acting president of Smith College, she was the unchallenged matriarch of the Morrow family. In each house, at mealtimes, she sat at the head of a long, polished table and dominated the room with her bright blue eyes and the soft white waves of her hair and the invisible buzzer under the carpet at her feet, for summoning The Servants.

At the other end of her table there was no grandfather, in

my time. Ambassador Dwight Whitney Morrow, banker and diplomat, to whom we children privately referred as "Grandpa Bee," had died many years before. And there was no "Uncle" in Grandma Bee's establishment, either. There was no man of the house at all, strictly speaking, though my grandmother did not live alone. Both in the winter home and on the summer island, and certainly in Mexico, too, although I never visited her there, she was surrounded by a rustling uniformed supporting army, The Servants. They were, like "The Romans" or "The Russians," a powerfully established entity in my mental world, making our grandmother's preferred way of life possible long past the era when her husband's social position had made it necessary, and making the comfort and joy of her twelve visiting grandchildren complete.

The Servants, I suspect, were at least partly responsible for Grandma Bee's unlimited tolerance for grandchildren at any time of the year. They were as much a part of my grandmother's family as our two other sets of maternal cousins, the Morrows (children of our mother's brother, Dwight Jr., and our Aunt Margot) and the Morgans (children of our mother's younger sister, Constance, and her husband, Aubrey). The seven Morrow and Morgan cousins visited our grandmother in the winter in New Jersey, as we did (in fact the Morrow family lived at Next Day Hill for several years, when the children were very young), and visited her again, as we did, during the great stretches of summer vacation, in Maine.

Indoors at Grandma Bee's establishments there were maids in black dresses with white aprons: Astrid, who had sand-colored hair; Gertrude, dark and sleek and seemly; and Carrie, a curly-headed brunette who was young, smiled at us, and had two perfectly round apple-red rouge spots on her soft cheeks, in a pretty, powdered face. There was also a butler, James, tall and exuberant, though he, too, dressed in black, and a cook,

Elsie, who handed out boxes of raisins to children if we visited her kitchen in New Jersey, and who let me walk right into the icebox once in Maine. It was not a sanitized steel walk-in refrigerator like others I have seen since, but a cold, wooden-paneled room, with many shelves but few windows, something like a cross between a meat locker and an ice-fishing shack. It was cooled by great blocks of ice that I remember as being half as tall as I was, and in perfect cubes. These individually were so substantial that the polar bear from *Beast, Bird, and Fish* could have sat upon one in comfort. The ice was delivered by truck and unloaded by the iceman with the aid of dark steel tongs at the back, kitchen entrance of the house, near the laundry line where white monogrammed sheets and towels flapped like sails in the summer winds.

Elsie had brown curly hair, a pale, smiling face, strong arms, and a knack for catching and cooking fish. When not making meals or supervising her kitchen, Elsie would put on a sun hat on summer afternoons, take a fishing rod and a can of bait, and go down to the rocky beach, where she would get in the rowboat that was left hauled up on the shore, and row out to fish for flounder in Penobscot Bay. Sometimes Astrid went with her, and sometimes my brother Jon.

Outdoors there was Ambrose, the chauffeur, with a reluctant look in his eye and a roughness to his voice. His was not so much a truly grim personality as a habitually grouchy one. And there were the gardeners, my favorite among them Owen Grant, from the island, who had a gentle face and a Maine accent that complemented the soft-spoken burr of his wife, Mary.

Mary Grant, Scottish by birth, had come over to this country as a young woman to take care of my Aunt Elisabeth, my mother's oldest sister and my Welsh Uncle Aubrey Morgan's first wife. Aunt Elisabeth had died young and beautiful in

1934, of pneumonia. Three years later, Aubrey married her much younger sister, my Aunt Con, and from this union came all the cousins with Welsh names: Saran, Rhidian, and Eiluned, as well as yet another Elisabeth. Although the reason for the distinction has never been made entirely clear to me, there are "s" Elisabeths (my cousin Saran's daughter) and "z" Elizabeths (my own daughter, Lizzy) scattered through our family to this day. There are also several Constances, and many variations of Anne (Anna, Susannah). My own name, Reeve, comes from an old surname in the Morrow family—there were Reeves, Spencers, and Cutters in the Morrow genealogy, and several of these names, like "Land" from my father's side, have been adopted as first names.

"Can't your family think of any women's names besides Constance, Elizabeth, and Anne?" a confused friend crossly asked one of my cousins not long ago. The answer is that we can and have, but there remains in the family an abiding loyalty to those three Morrow sisters and their mother. Something about these small, strong women, held in affection over the generations, makes their daughters and granddaughters look at our own newborn daughters with respect, awe, and that intergenerational astonishment that comes to women who have just given birth. And so we repeat those names: Elizabeth (Elisabeth), and Constance, and Anne.

15
Con and Aubrey

※ ALTHOUGH many people acquainted with the family history have considered the story of Elisabeth and Aubrey a romantic one, I for one have never thought that dying young counted for much in the way of romance, and I suspect that Aunt Elisabeth would agree with me. The story of Con and Aubrey, on the other hand—now, there was romance for you! I imagined the lonely widower lingering in the comforting company of his wife's younger siblings during those first few years after her death. Perhaps he already had a special feeling for Constance, the baby of the family, loving and loyal and tradition-minded, like her mother. Perhaps he watched with increasing interest as she grew up, becoming a brilliant student with a down-to-earth manner, and a twinkle in her eye. Then suddenly, some weekend when she came home from college, it hit him—Constance! How could he have been so blind!

In some of my daydreams Aunt Con is coming down the stairs to greet Aubrey on this fateful weekend. Aubrey comes in through the front door at Next Day Hill, and crosses the vast and shiny tiled hall. He looks up, and there she is, moving in his direction, and all at once he *knows* . . . I played the scene over and over in my mind, and it was equally satisfying each time, though sometimes a little different in detail. There might be a glowering storm, with wind and clouds, and Uncle Aubrey would arrive drenched, and troubled at heart, with water dripping onto the floor from a big, black, British umbrella, which James, or an earlier James, would remove from his grasp with deft discretion, to prevent it from dripping on the carpets.

Uncle Aubrey was large, thoughtful, and astute, a lover of symphonies and of Saki (the writer H. H. Munro, not the Japanese alcohol, as far as I know). He was a focus of my attention whenever I was in his presence, because I thought him not only extraordinarily well educated and well informed, but also very funny. I remember his Welsh accent and his deep, echoing laughter. He laughed until his face got red and the tears came, and it was impossible not to laugh with him. I remember his Panama hat, in summers in Maine, and the red bandanna he wore tied around his neck during the years when he and Aunt Con, having left behind them the foreign service and diplomatic life in London and Washington, raised beef cattle on a farm at the confluence of the Columbia and the Lewis Rivers near Ridgefield, Washington.

The farm was called "Plas Newydd," or "New Place," in Welsh. The two "d"s of Newydd were pronounced "th" in Welsh, causing mispronunciations like "Plas Nood" or "Plath Newth" to come easily from the unwary. From their farm, on clear days, they could see Mount St. Helens in the distance, snow-swept and peaceful-looking during the years before its volcanic eruption, like Mount Fuji in a Japanese print.

The Morgans raised their children on the farm and sent them to school in nearby Ridgefield, where Aunt Con was elected to the school board. Later, the Morgan children went east for boarding school and college, and came back again with summer crowds of cousins and college friends to bale hay and drive tractors with Uncle Aubrey, and help Aunt Con cook for the farm. She and Uncle Aubrey sent the whole crew off in midsummer, though, to attend the Shakespeare Festival in Ashland, Oregon, at night, and to run the Rogue River rapids on inner tubes by day.

Most of all, this aunt and uncle inspired confidence. "If you can read, you can cook," Aunt Con reassured her niece and namesake, Connie Morrow, who arrived for a summer at Plas Newydd with little experience in the kitchen. Aunt Con made us feel, in fact, that if you could read, you could do anything. On the other hand, you did not necessarily have to.

"Let's not, and say we did!" she would suggest, with a smile and a tilted chin, in response to some distasteful social engagement, although she did not miss many of these. Like her mother before her, she was small, active, energetic, and positive. Beyond the farm life, Aunt Con was a scholar and a writer. Her book about her mother, Elizabeth Morrow, was published under the title *A Distant Moment,* in 1978. Always interested in education, Aunt Con, like her mother before her, served as president of the board of trustees of Smith College and was as active as her predecessor on behalf of their shared alma mater. Wherever she lived, her home was a magnet for young people: a place of good food and good conversation, laughter and books and children and dogs.

"Our Lady of the Canines," a friend of the family referred to her, after long experience of tripping over Corgis and Labradors and, one year, because of an unsupervised moment, an improbable and ungainly combination the family called "Corgidors."

It seemed to me that Aunt Con's spirit, like her house, was generous alike to past and present. There was in one quiet room at Plas Newydd a portrait of Aunt Elisabeth, painted shortly before she died, hanging above the fireplace.

It counted greatly with me, romance and history aside, that Uncle Aubrey had married not one but two of the Morrow sisters, demonstrating a sincere, lifelong allegiance to the family.

I think, though, that what I appreciated in Uncle Aubrey most of all was his friendship with my father. This never appeared to waver or abate, though the two men must have had severe differences in outlook before the Second World War. Aubrey was then a representative of the British government and my father a staunch and controversial isolationist, who believed that for the U.S. to join in the war effort in an attempt to save England would be futile. The impression he gave in his speeches was that England, irresolute and ill-prepared, was already a lost cause.

"Your father never really understood the British character," Uncle Aubrey said to me once after my father's death, with a small, forgiving smile. According to my uncle, nothing in Charles Lindbergh's upbringing or education could help him comprehend the forces that drove the British to victory, against all odds, in the Battle of Britain, and changed the course of the war.

When they met as brothers-in-law and uncles, in the 1950s and 1960s, I could hear the two of them rumbling through political discussions during long evenings at our house in Connecticut whenever the Morgans visited. One night at the height of the Cuban Missile Crisis, under President Kennedy, we all sat around the radio in the living room in Darien together and waited to hear what would happen. Because there was no television in our household, my father and Uncle Aubrey talked, then listened, then talked, while my mother and Aunt Con worried, and sat back and listened, and watched the men.

The sound of the news that night had an urgent, frightening quality to it, with music rolling like low thunder between the broadcasts. We waited for hours. Nobody knew what the outcome would be of Kennedy's insistence that Soviet missiles be removed from Cuba.

My father and my uncle were both large men. Because of their physical bulk and their experiences, they fully occupied the room. They sat and listened, and sat and talked, with the felt entitlement of their size. They seemed to shoulder heavier responsibilities, and to breathe greater quantities of oxygen, than the rest of us. I watched them all evening, passing the fragile peace of the world back and forth to one another as if it were a pipe across a campfire.

I had grown up with civil defense drills in school—the alarm sounded, then we all put our pencils down neatly and crouched beside our desks in what was thought at that time to be adequate preparation for a nuclear attack. I had heard a lot about Communists, and about "Old Joe Stalin," as my father called the Russian leader. I had seen pictures of soldiers marching in Red Square in *Life* magazine, and I had had dreams of Russians marching up our driveway, crunch crunch crunching across the gravel right past the rhododendrons, rows of goose-stepping dark figures wearing red stars. I confused Communists with Nazis in my dreams, and confused both of them with cannibals (we subscribed to the *National Geographic*). In one dream all of these groups were dancing around a fire in our driveway together, with bones in their noses, after having cut me and the rest of the family up into little pieces and thrown us into a barrel. It wasn't as bad as it sounds. From our vantage point, well hidden and all mixed up indistinguishably together, we were still a family, and we could still watch the dance.

But the dreams of my childhood were much less frightening than the long wait by the radio that evening. My feelings about the Russians and the Missile Crisis were a nightmare of fear, ignorance, and excessive imagination, but Uncle Aubrey reassured me.

"The Russians," he said, "are a ponderous, bearlike people." He did not think they would act so precipitately during the Missile Crisis as to start a Third World War. My father was not so sure, but I believed my uncle, who had had considerably more political experience. He was, besides, somewhat bearlike himself. I thought he was in a position to know what he was talking about. Because of Uncle Aubrey, when I finally went upstairs to bed that night, I could fall asleep. In the morning, sure enough, the world was still safe, and the Russians were backing off. I could now imagine them doing it, not in the uniforms of skinny goose-steppers, but with the deliberate, ponderous movements of bears.

16
Grandma Bee

✳ W HEN our family visited Grandma Bee during the winter, we went to Englewood, New Jersey, to a residence that is now the Elisabeth Morrow School, a private school named for the same Aunt Elisabeth who was Uncle Aubrey's first wife. Back then, as I've mentioned, the property was called Next Day Hill, and the name, like the name of my grandmother's house in Mexico, Casa Mañana, was a play on her own name, Morrow, a little frivolity of which, along with many other things about the family, I was not aware until long after her death. I only knew that we would often go to Grandma Bee's house, only an hour's drive from our own, for Sunday dinner, and that we would dress and behave very well on these occasions. We would also, inexplicably, bring the dog.

All of us, including the dog, were impeccable at the start of the journey. We were arranged in my father's organized fashion inside our Ford Ranch Wagon, the automobile my father had chosen for suburban family life. This car was long, ample, and utilitarian, and on the outside it was painted a color he called "gun-metal gray." I remember my father's satisfaction in picking out the color when he was studying the available models in the Ford company's brochure. My father may have chosen it in one more attempt to camouflage and conceal his family from the world, a vehicle that mixed family travel with protection, part covered wagon and part battleship. Or maybe his choice was tinged by the memory of his work as a consultant for Henry Ford during World War II, when the automaker was building airplanes in Dearborn, Michigan.

My father, in the driver's seat, wore his navy pinstripe suit. He handed over to us, in the back seat, his gray fedora to hold and keep safe during the drive; woe betide any child who mislaid or—much worse—sat on his hat. My mother, beside him, wore a cotton print dress by Lanz of Austria, often with a belt at the waist and always with pockets. She felt that a belt, or "sash," gave a dress more shape and style. Many was the time I stood uncertainly in front of a long mirror in the "Young Miss" section of a department store, Bloomingdale's, Best's, or Bonwit's, having tried on an unsuccessful-looking new dress from one of the racks, while my mother behind me murmured, encouragingly, "Perhaps with a sash . . ."

My mother liked to have pockets in all of her clothes, too, in case one of her children needed a handkerchief, but also in order to conceal there a stone, a shiny horse chestnut, or another treasure to fondle in secret, with her smooth warm moving fingers. She had an absentminded way of tearing and folding airline luggage tags into an elaborate system of triangles, complicated as the "cootie-catchers" we made with our friends from school, those little finger-fitted fortune-telling devices on which we penciled numbers and colors and boys' names, and after a series of leading questions could tell our best friends, "You will marry Peter, and have two girls and three boys, and all of the children's eyes will be blue." But although we labored over these, folding and refolding them many times to make our cootie-catchers come out just right, my mother did her paper-folding without even looking at it, and with one hand. I could never figure out how she did this.

She was not proud of her skill a bit, and if I made the mistake of admiring it, she would show a startled self-disgust, and throw away the folded tag she was working on. I could not figure this out, either. I thought the tags were as exquisite as origami, with an ordered, intricate beauty in their tattered folds.

On the drive to New Jersey, a thick bright wool Mexican hair ribbon might be threaded in her dark hair, or a thin black velvet one, and at the neck of her dress there would be a pin: a cameo with flowers painted on it, a silver heart, or a golden reproduction of a scallop shell, companion to one that Aunt Con had, in silver.

The back seats of the Ranch Wagon were fresh with the clean combed hair of the brothers and the cotton print dresses and bow-tied-in-back sashes of the sisters. But behind us all, like a threatening cloud in slow pursuit, was the shadowy nervousness of our handsome young German shepherd, Sigurd, or Siggy. He was unhappy and uncertain from the very beginning of the drive. First he paced back and forth, whining, then he stretched out, forlorn with disorientation, across the floor behind the back seats. He was surrounded by several thicknesses of newspapers, spread out to cover every surface with which he might come in contact. The dog was an uneasy traveler, and tended to throw up about the time we got to the George Washington Bridge.

This bridge, and the lighthouse tucked in beneath it as a warning guide to tugboats and barges plying the Hudson River, were a focus of excited anticipation for me, as they were the main characters in a story our mother used to read to us at bedtime, called *The Little Red Lighthouse and the Great Gray Bridge*. Each time we got close to the bridge, on the way to our grandmother's Sunday dinner in New Jersey, I would press my face hard against the window and look up into the sky as far as I could, to make sure that the Great Gray Bridge was still as great and as gray as it had been in the story, and it always was. Then immediately, knowing that it might be too late to catch a glimpse of it at all, I would stretch and twist my neck around and down as far as I could behind us, to make sure that the Little Red Lighthouse was still there below the bridge, just as little and red as ever. And it always was. Finally, at about the time I had verified that everything was as it should be, and just as I was settling back and relaxing into my seat once again, we would take the turn onto the George Washington Bridge itself, and the dog, with an apologetic groan, would vomit. The vomit —I remember this very clearly because I have never seen anything like it before or since—was always green.

We children would gather up the soiled newspapers and stuff them in a bag out of sight and scent, spread some new clean newspapers around the humiliated and mournful Sigurd, and drive on into New Jersey. Eventually we reached the quiet, tree-shaded town of Englewood, where we would soon hear the squeaky sound of bricks under our tires, and shortly afterward the slowing of the Ranch Wagon and the sudden smell of box bushes would signal our arrival at Next Day Hill.

Of the Sunday dinner itself, I can only remember the taste of roast beef and Yorkshire pudding, and that taste melts still in my mouth in my dreams, though it has never been the same afterward in real life. My grandmother's dining room was bigger than ours at home, with two doors opening into it from the hallway and another, swinging door at the opposite side of the room near the kitchen. Through this James would emerge again and again, with trays of food shoulder-high, one course after another, and never drop anything on anybody. The swinging door through which he came and went had a little round porthole in it at an adult's eye level. I imagined someone always stationed immediately behind it, his or her assignment to look into the dining room and judge the children's behavior.

On our side of this door, just behind my grandmother's chair, there stood a tall folded screen, covered with painted pictures of rivers and trees and horses and clouds. I suppose it must have been there to shield the diners from kitchen noises, but at the time it didn't seem to have a purpose, and was for me just one more of the many unexplained adornments that accompanied my grandmother through space, planets in her universe of treasures.

The table itself had a big bowl of flowers sitting in the very center, and flowers also floated in the finger bowls that were placed in front of us toward the end of the meal (although sometimes, wonderfully, there were instead little wooden ducks, like miniature decoys, floating there as if on a crystal pond, with all their markings perfectly painted by the smallest brush in the world). Near where I sat there was a fish made of silver, about six inches in length, and hinged somehow inside so that it was supple to the touch. It was irresistible, so ingeniously made that I could wiggle its tail slightly with one finger and it would move from side to side in a sinuous, fishlike way upon the polished darkness of the table, shine reflecting shine. Each place setting had a white napkin with my grandmother's initials printed on it in blue—ECM, only the M was in the middle, and larger than the other two letters, so that it really read EMC, which mystified me. The napkins were made of paper, and if you very carefully separated one from the other, you would discover that there were six thin layers of paper forming each napkin, although all except the top layer, with the monogram, were plain white. Instead of a salt shaker there was a little silver pot with a tiny indigo blue glass bowl full of salt nested inside it, at each place. This whole arrangement was no bigger than the glass eye cup of the same color that stood on the shelf of my mother's medicine cabinet at home, although the cup on Grandma Bee's dining table had a silver spoon inside it, for sprinkling salt onto food the way sugar was shoveled into a bowl of cereal. I learned this by watching the adults at the table, though I did not often use the salt myself. Still, I liked the spoon very much. It looked as if it would have been the perfect size and shape for a soup ladle for a mouse.

There was a confusing array of silver knives and forks and spoons bordering each dinner plate, both to right and left, and on the plate itself either a painted yellow tulip, or a primrose, or even a rose. A rose was the rarest flower. If you sat down at Grandma Bee's table and found yourself in front of a plate with a rose on it, you were the envy of all the other cousins.

Aside from the dining room, on the ground floor of my grandmother's house, there was the hall, on one side opening into "Aunt Elisabeth's Blue Room," as we called the little study where her portrait hung, near a sofa that was upholstered in the same muted robin's-egg color as the walls. These had lightly painted on them a series of bamboolike branches on which many colored painted birds were perched. This room was exactly opposite from another, contrastingly masculine-looking study that had a painting of Grandpa Bee on the wall and an atmosphere of red leather and mahogany.

Down at the far end of the tiled hallway there was a living room with a fireplace and armchairs and a table for afternoon tea, which my grandmother dispensed to her grandchildren with milk or lemon, and as many sugar cubes as we could manage to select with the aid of a pair of silver sugar tongs. There were cinnamon toast triangles arranged plentifully on a plate, and a fire burning in the fireplace. Grandma Bee presided kindly over the selection.

Beyond that room of dusk and comfort there was a kind of

porch or sun room, with glass-topped tables and flowered cushions on lightweight furniture giving a feeling of summer weather and easy living. On a table in that room there was a glass case the size of a shoebox, crowded with multicolored birds no bigger than my thumb, bright scraps of feather and silk as sudden and still as a flock of hummingbirds frozen in mid-flight.

Farther on, there was an enormous, formal room that I rarely entered, as it was never occupied and seemed reserved for grand events I was too young to attend, funerals or fancy-dress balls. Leading to a far wing of Next Day Hill there was an open area known as the Mexican Room, and here there were Mexican paintings on the walls, and bright pots on shelves. Nearby, in a corridor, there was a dollhouse we could play with, fully furnished and with stairs that went all the way up through the ceiling, to the second floor. The stairs in Anne's and my dollhouse at home stopped at the ceiling, to our disappointment, with no opening at the top. How were the dolls supposed to get upstairs? It was annoying to hop or fly them up in our fingers when we were playing: it broke the spell. The dollhouse at Grandma Bee's, with the furniture and staircase in the right places, and of the right size, made the miniature and imaginary world so precisely faithful to the larger, more real one that the transition between the two was smooth and unbroken, and the magic remained.

The physical environment of my grandmother's house was an enchantment in itself, the light and glide and shine and sparkle of it: the polished floors—both tile and wood—the glistening tabletops, the deep, soft armchairs, the flowers, the fireplaces, the sense that you could start at one end of a room, run three steps and then slide for a mile before you came to the opposite wall. The real staircase at Grandma Bee's, like the doll's staircase, was thoroughly satisfactory. It curved in a broad spiral up the back wall, like a staircase ascending to a ballroom for Cinderella. And for those who did not climb stairs, there was a private elevator, with a brass grillwork door that opened and closed in the manner of an accordion. On one of the inner walls there was a brightly painted picture of Benjamin Franklin flying a kite, on another a mirror decorated with balloons. Electricity, buoyancy, and my grandmother's laughter accompanied the riders silently up to the second floor.

Upstairs at Next Day Hill, most of what I remember is white. If we stayed overnight, on beyond our Sunday dinner visit, we slept upon and among crisp, white, well-ironed pillowcases and sheets, with white lace-edged scarves on our bureaus and light muslin curtains at the windows. There was white-painted nursery furniture in my room, and there were white wicker laundry hampers in the bathroom, where steaming hot water flowed into a deep white claw-footed bathtub from white porcelain-handled taps, on which the "H" and the "C" for Hot and Cold looked as if they had been engraved by Tiffany's. After a bath, and drying off with a white-and-blue towel monogrammed exactly like the napkins, EMC, I would climb into bed and fall into a cloudlike sleep with the smell of box bushes drifting in the windows, and the sounds of footsteps—one of the maids, Carrie? Astrid? Or was it my grandmother, presiding even to the end of the day and to the very edge of consciousness?—tapping away gently down the hall.

17
To the Island

✳ I N the summer, we started our journey toward this same grandmother on the train, in Connecticut, just as we did when we went to see Farmor and Uncle in Detroit. This time, though, we rode north, on the Bar Harbor Express, with its portly uniformed conductors who never spoke but only sang, like opera stars, announcing the name of each town as we approached it with a flourish from the entrance to the train car where we sat, and a great rush of air from the open door—"NorWALK," "NORwalk next . . . NEW Canaan . . ." They sang us all the way up the eastern seaboard to Rockland, Maine, where we were met by my grandmother's car, driven by the implacable Ambrose.

My mind's eye now dresses Ambrose in a gray tweed jacket, and boots, and a cap like a gamekeeper's on some vast estate in Great Britain, but I think my mind's eye has developed delusions of grandeur. Ambrose in my memory anyway is solid, gray, grumpy, and in tweeds, even in summertime. Enveloped by his subduing presence and the deep smell of leather seats, we were driven in style through Rockland, where before we could see anything significant, we could already sense our freedom and the sea.

We wound circuitously through the town along narrow

streets, past the Farnsworth museum, past Woolworth's Five-and-Ten-Cent-Store, and down to the public landing. There we were met amid the hoots of the incoming ferries and the cries of seagulls and the sights and smells of raw fish and seaweed and outboard motors and creosote-covered wharf pilings by Captain Stone. The Captain was a noble-looking, taciturn island resident whose tight jaw and lean physique commanded respect. He captained a boat called *The Mouette*. This boat in fact had belonged in my family since my own parents had taken it on their honeymoon in 1929, almost a quarter of a century earlier. It was built by the ELCO company, owned by the family of Harold Bixby, one of the original businessmen sponsors of the *Spirit of St. Louis* flight in 1927. Still I thought of it as the Captain's. Also, as I was not to learn French for many years, I did not understand that "mouette" meant "seagull." Instead I associated the name of the boat vaguely with the herds of Holsteins and Jerseys I had seen through the train window as we made our way north, and I sat lulled and soothed all the way across the bay to the island by the drone of the boat's motor and the braided liquid patterns of the wake we left behind us, feeling tired but safe in the protective custody of a benign, oceangoing bovinity.

Even before we got to the island, just in the trip across the bay from Rockland, everything from our winter and mainland life started to dissolve into a dreamlike equivalency of water and sun and summer days. It was a place and a time in my life when the outward order of things, established by Grandma Bee so wholeheartedly, provided an inward liberty that was all mine. I felt it in the vibrations of the motor, and in Captain Stone's steady competence at the helm, and again as I rubbed my hands along the varnished wood of the rail to feel the shine, or watched the salt spray leap up before us to meet the bow of the boat. I knew it as I passed two- or even three-masted schooners traveling in their stately way along the horizon, setting a rhythm for the season that can only truly be set by sail. I recognized it in the cormorants gathered in loitering gangly groups on the rocks at the entrance to the harbor, drying their wings like ragged bits of laundry in the wind, and in the sight of the lobster buoys of all colors bobbing in the Fox Island Thoroughfare, the channel between North Haven and Vinalhaven. I felt it settle in for the whole summer as we finally nosed into our own mooring near the Casino wharf, among sailboats big and small.

The trip to the island now, by ferry, to visit the cousins who have inherited Aunt Con's property there, has the same effect upon me that it did forty-five years ago, in my grandmother's boat. This is a summer journey my family has taken for generations, in order to experience liberation and belonging at exactly the same time.

In her book *North to the Orient* (New York, Harcourt Brace, 1935) my mother wrote about coming back to North Haven this way:

As we neared our geographical destination we were also nearing our emotional one. The last lap of the journey across to the island by small boat completed both of these ends and each familiar personal landmark, drawing from us always the same exclamations —"The four-masted schooner is still there!" "Isn't that the five-mile buoy?" "There's our big spruce tree!"—linked us at last completely and satisfactorily to all past summers—to all vacations and to Maine.

I remember my childhood summers on North Haven as the lightest, brightest vacations of my life. The remaining visions of them are as bleached and indistinct as overexposed photographs, shot through with sunlight and salt air, haunted by happiness, peopled largely with women and children. In this matriarchal stronghold of the Morrows, as at Next Day Hill, the men of the family were as welcome as any of the other visiting dignitaries, but the women were in charge.

The other day, in some photocopied family papers my brother Land sent to me, I came across my grandmother's notes on the building of the house in Maine. The site on the former property of an island resident, Deacon Brown, for whom the point was named, and the new house looked westward across Penobscot Bay toward Camden. My grandmother wrote this in her journal on July 26, 1927, the day of the ground-breaking,

It was a perfect day, the Camden Hills blue and beautiful.

It was barely two months since my father had landed the *Spirit of St. Louis* in Paris, and half a year before my mother met him for the first time, in Mexico City. I can imagine the bright clarity of July in North Haven, and can see the rocky shore and feel the wind. I am thinking now that if my grandmother had a clear view of Camden that day, she must have seen the four islands, too, halfway across the water that stretched between where she stood and where the towns, Rockland and Camden, had grown up on the other side of the bay. I memorized the alliterative litany of their names, Mark, Saddle, LaSalle, and Lyme, early on, when the sounds of words were often much more important to me than their meaning. In the same way, Colorado, Casco Bay, and Abilene still thrill me for reasons that have nothing to do with actual experience in any of those locations. The four islands, which I have never visited, resonate in my understanding like the names of saints in a childhood prayer. For me it was not "Matthew, Mark, Luke, and John," but Mark, Saddle, LaSalle, and Lyme, who were the gospel-makers of my summers, forming a physical and spiritual horizon that always floated just beyond my reach. They gave to my days a peace that passed my understanding, this landscape of resting lumps upon the water, with the paler blue of the Camden Hills fading away behind them.

It seems to me that we borrowed the name "Saddle" and gave it to a favorite sitting branch on the old apple tree that grew near my grandmother's kitchen. It must have been there since the Deacon's time. Its rotting places were tarred over in our day to encourage healing, its ailing upper limbs tied together with taut black cables over which my brother Land once tried to tightrope, and failed, and fell to the ground hard, landing on an apple and knocking the wind out of himself, but not breaking any bones. All the same, he lay still enough to prompt our cousin Rhidian to rush into my grandmother's living room, where she and some other summer ladies were playing cards. There Rhidian danced and screamed in his summer shorts and little blue sneakers, with the bloodthirsty exuberance called forth by another child's disaster. His words, "Land's dead! Land's dead!" reverberated throughout the shaded safety of my grandmother's house.

We climbed and played and swam and sailed through those summers, and walked the beaches, and played together and alone on the rocks, by the sea, in the shelter of the spruce trees and the pines. We found brambly patches of wild raspberries and struggled through them late in the summer with everbloodier elbows, knees, and wrists, reaching for just one—and then just one more—sweet risky mouthful of fruit. Would there be a tiny black bug inside this bite of raspberry, as there was in the last one, or would it turn out to be a speck of dirt? We spat out the bugs, but we considered Maine dirt to be cleaner than ours at home in Connecticut, or in New York or Washington, and fully digestible.

There was not much wildlife—rabbits occasionally hopped across the lawn, and gulls wheeled and turned over our heads, raucous in the wind. Occasionally the slippery head of a harbor seal could be seen bobbing up in the water, if it wasn't a piece of driftwood instead, as it too often proved to be. And forever there was that same invisible, discreet, and wistfully repeating song of the white-throated sparrow in the summer air.

We were told by our elders that the sparrow sang "Old Sam Peabody, Peabody, Peabody," in its perpetual three-part refrain, but I never learned who Old Sam Peabody was. Did he summer on North Haven? Did he have an account at Waterman's, the General Store? How old *was* he? As old as my grandmother with her wavy white hair and her golfing hat and her blue eyes, her face as indicative of character as an outcropping of Maine granite, and yet at the same time as gently wrinkled and softly scented as her own snapdragons? As old as Owen Grant, the gardener, who could not have been much older than my mother, or my Aunt Con, at the time, but who seemed ancient in his khaki shirt and trousers, his omnipresence in the garden? Owen was responsible for the rock gardens and the perennial borders and the snapdragons, but not the dandelions. Dandelions were a scourge, in Grandma Bee's eye, the one plant which we were allowed to dig up and root out of her lawn anytime we found it. She even put a price on it, and her grandchildren as bounty hunters could sell dandelions to her for a penny a plant.

High above the dandelions, and above the lawn and the garden, sea-salted and wind-blessed, my grandmother's house floated free as a square-rigged sail in coastal fog, or baked quietly as a barnacle on a rock in the paint-blistering sunshine of an August noon. The house gave honor to her sloping well-tended gardens, where bees hummed ominously in the snap-dragons as I hurried past them on the way to the beach, to her perennial borders whose edges were trimmed as neatly as if cut with the scissors I used for making paper dolls, to the stands of pine and spruce that grew far out beyond the gardens along the bluffs, and which unlike the gardens were allowed to run their own way, disorderly as we twelve cousins, the grandchil-dren, in the wind and salt air.

When my grandmother's house was sold, my Aunt Con kept the "Little House," a cottage built on the same property but separated by a wooded patch from the larger one. The "Little House" had been built originally as a private retreat for my grandmother's three daughters, Elisabeth, Anne, and Con-stance, with support and funding by their father, Dwight W. Morrow. The sisters decided together that they needed one place in their lives that was separated from their mother's ener-getic social schedule, a place where each young woman could pursue her own quieter interests. Their father, an unusually liberated man for his day and age, thoroughly approved. Elisa-beth was planning a school for young children, my mother wanted to write, and Aunt Con, when asked what her own interests might be, declared that she wanted to cook! It was Con, scholar, writer, and pioneer in women's education, who chose the furnishings, set up the kitchen, and ultimately loved and used the house more than either of her sisters did. It has always seemed to me that the Little House was destined to be hers, from the very beginning. Con came back to North Haven every summer, with Aubrey while he lived and then with her children and grandchildren until she died in 1995. My sister Anne rented a house close by and spent summers on the island, too, in the mid-1980s, with her children. From Deacon Brown's Point, after a troubled period following a divorce, Anne wrote this poem:

North Haven—June 20

This much is sure—
that I am here again
at the morning window in another year
as are the wings, the birdsong
and the line of firs against the sky,
the line of winter tides along the beach
and streaks of calm smoothing the ruffled bay.
The things that change the least
Are those that never are the same
But are always there.
Endure, return, endure—
And do not compare.

Anne was married for the third time, in 1988, to author and Dartmouth professor Noel Perrin. They had several years of peace and happiness together in Vermont before she became ill for the second time with cancer. When we scattered Anne's ashes on the beach in North Haven in the summer of 1994, it seemed the best place for this ceremony, and it seemed right to me that there was no longer any separation between my sister and those wings, those firs, that birdsong, that bay, and the open ocean beyond.

18
Inaccessible Parents

✳ T H E earlier generation's pair of sisters, my mother and Aunt Con, met many times in Maine, at Aunt Con's house, during the summers in the 1980s and 1990s. Sometimes my mother would visit our family in Vermont for a few days first, and I would drive her to the ferry dock in Rockland, and take the ferry ride across the bay with her to spend a day or two on North Haven before going back to the farm. The drive to Rockland from my home took us east through the mountains of New Hampshire past Gorham to Bethel, and across Maine's midriff through the inland wooded counties of Oxford, Androscoggin, and Kennebec. We drove through old established summer communities of gray-shingled mansions in the White Mountains, and through hardscrabble backwoods Maine hamlets consisting of no more than a scattering of trailers and machine sheds. We went around lakes ringed with tourist cabins, and followed the Grand Trunk railway line, now little used, through lonely stretches of boggy wetland, then past hillside farms that looked as if they had produced more rocks than crops in their fields for two centuries. We motored sedately through the white clapboard, picture-postcard-perfect village of Wayne, Maine, and sped on into Augusta with its high bridges and confusing traffic circles, where we finally turned onto Route 17, and followed it all the way across Knox County, to Rockland.

"As we neared our geographical destination we were also nearing our emotional one." When we drove together to North Haven in the summer of 1989, my mother talked throughout the drive about her own mother, my Grandma Bee, in a way I had not heard before. My mother was eighty-three years old, and I, her daughter, was not much more than half her age. She did not talk to me that day as if I were her daughter, though. She spoke as if we were contemporaries, even siblings, as if I were yet another, slightly younger, Morrow sister. It may be that she was anticipating her weekend with Aunt Con, or perhaps our two identities were already blurring a little in her mind, as they do now.

She was airing old complaints, and revealing unhealed wounds, during those four hours. I had always known that my mother had wanted to go to Bryn Mawr College, back in the 1920s, but had finally decided to go to Smith instead, at the urging of Aunt Elisabeth. Her sister told her that to attend any college but Smith would "hurt" their mother. I did not know until that drive to Maine how bitterly my mother minded her own capitulation, even though she had enjoyed her years at Smith. Now I heard all about it, and felt with her both the pull of family loyalty and the stab of personal disappointment.

I knew, too, that Grandma Bee had enjoyed playing golf—there was a meadow at Deacon Brown's Point that she had turned into a golf course, a long stretch of grass running down to the beach. I did not know, though, that when Grandma Bee had given her own children golf lessons, my mother had hated the sport. "Because it is so introspective; you have too much time to think!" she complained resentfully in my car. I was surprised, because I had always imagined that introspection was my mother's native tongue, and that "time to think" had

been a precious, rare commodity all her life. I listened to her
complaints with fascination, and sympathy, and little comment.
I had so rarely heard her complain at all, and never about her
mother.

Most of all, I was surprised and disconcerted to hear my
mother tell me that she had often thought of her parents as
"inaccessible," a word I had not heard her use before this
conversation. Anne and I had used it quite recently, though,
and more than once, when discussing together the preoccupations and busy lives of our own father and mother during the
time we were growing up. They were so involved with their
work, their travels, their writing, we had said to each other. He
was physically, she emotionally absent for long stretches at a
time, we had decided. After our conversation I had thought
about all the family trips we took together, and about our
father teaching us to swim and to drive, about his reading *The
Jungle Book* out loud on winter evenings in front of the living
room fire. I thought about the time when I was sick in bed
with an earache, and my mother came and sat with me all
afternoon without saying a word, in my darkened bedroom,
and held my hand. I thought of all these times and became
uneasy, and I was uneasy now, again, listening to my mother.
Her complaints about her parents were so familiar that they
threw me back on myself. I wondered about this cry of "inac-
cessibility." Is it universal? What is it about? Is it true that all
parents are too busy to pay full attention to their children? Or
is the truth instead that no child can ever be satisfied, because
no child can have every ounce of a parent's attention? Do we
all imagine ourselves, whether we are teenagers, middle-aged,
or octogenarians, as insufficiently appreciated children? When
my children talk to each other, the way Anne and I did, do
they voice these same complaints? And will their children say
the same?

As soon as my mother and I got to Aunt Con's house on the island, the old atmosphere was restored. There were the raspberry bushes and the pine trees, the white paint and the green shutters, the window boxes and the rock gardens spilling over with flowers, the old apple tree blooming just outside the window and the green bench against the wall. In the evening, my mother in her pink sweater and Aunt Con in her blue one sat together side by side on the bench and watched the sun go down over the Camden hills, before dinner.

Inside the Little House there were traces of my grandmother, still: the china on the shelves and the framed embroidery on the walls, samplers worked by nineteenth-century children, things Grandma Bee had collected a generation ago. There were toby jugs on the mantelpieces, and a ship in a bottle on a table in the living room, and there were little leather-bound books with tiny print on bookcases just the right size to accommodate them. In the bathrooms there was still the white wicker furniture I remembered, and the claw-footed tubs with porcelain taps, and on the towel rods the same monogrammed towels, with the same monogram, EMC, Elizabeth Cutter Morrow. I was surprised to see this, rather than a new monogram for Aunt Con, whose initials would have read CMM. Could these have been the same towels I used as a child, forty years before? Had there been an infinite amount of household linen ordered in my grandmother's day, and then stored away for posterity? Or had these been reproduced on purpose by her daughter Constance in the 1980s, in her memory, another complicated act of generosity toward the past? I never knew.

My mother and her sister remembered their childhood together that evening with laughter. They told me about the family dog, Daffin, that had tried to swim back across the Rio Grande during the first trip to Mexico—"The only one in the family with any sense!" one of their uncles had remarked. They recalled the amorous, very young tutor, Mr. Jakum, who had been hired to teach the children, but who fell in love with Grandma Bee's sister, Annie Cutter. Aunt Annie had never married and was in her forties during Mr. Jakum's tenure. She found his attentions so absurd that she wrote verses about him, which my mother and Aunt Con both could still recite, giggling:

> This poor fool asks, "How old are you?"
> I say to him, "Too old for you!"

When they remembered their fencing lessons together, my mother stood up and mimicked the stances they had been taught, one hand on her hip, the other brandishing an invisible épée, and Aunt Con chuckled from her sofa by the fire. They told the story of their meeting with President Calvin Coolidge, which had caused Aunt Con deep mortification, because he had looked at her and said to Grandma Bee, "Why, she looks just like Hilda!" Their Aunt Hilda, their father's sister, was by then middle-aged and fat. Con learned only later that Hilda had been a beauty, and much admired by the future President in her youth. They talked about Grandma Cutter and Grandma Foote, and tried to identify for me their relatives on each side of the family. They traced "the Cutter connection" easily, but "the Foote connection" was more difficult. Together, out loud, my mother and her sister racked their brains for Foote names, forgetting and remembering one relative after another, this Foote's father and that Foote's wife, a Foote brother and a Foote niece, sounding eventually like a couple of demented podiatrists, and laughing until the light was gone and the fire was low, and it was time for bed.

I have a photograph of the two sisters together in Maine, sitting in a lobster boat, heading for a picnic on one of the

White Islands in Penobscot Bay. Con in a blue raincoat is smiling at my mother in a pink sweater. My mother's hand is at her throat, holding the ends of her patterned scarf in place—it looks as if the wind is blowing across the deck of the boat—and there is a look of ecstasy on her face.

"As we neared our geographical destination . . ."

Two or three times a summer, during Aunt Con's last years, my mother would visit Aunt Con in North Haven. In the winter, Aunt Con would visit my mother in Florida, at a condominium in Fort Myers Beach where my mother still goes regularly to be near her lifelong friends, Jim and Ellie Newton. It was the Newtons who found the place on Captiva Island where my mother lived and walked and wrote *Gift from the Sea* in 1955. Aunt Con had come to see her that winter, too. In one of the chapters of her book my mother characterizes the relationship of sisters as one that "can illustrate the essence of relationships," an understanding companionship of two complete and independent individuals who choose to be together.

We wash the dishes lightly to no system, for there are not enough to matter. We work easily and instinctively together, not bumping into each other as we go back and forth about our tasks. We talk as we sweep, as we dry, as we put away, discussing a person or a poem or a memory. And since our communication seems more important to us than our chores, the chores are done without thinking. . . . We walk up the beach in silence, but in harmony, as the sandpipers ahead of us move like a corps of ballet dancers keeping time to some rhythm inaudible to us. Intimacy is blown away. Emotions are carried out to sea. We are even free of thoughts, at least of their articulation; clean and bare as whitened driftwood; empty as shells, ready to be filled up again with the impersonal sea and sky and wind.

Forty years later, when they spent time together again in Florida, my mother and her sister were still, clearly, two very distinct individuals, still resembling one another: small, careful, blue-eyed, dignified, and alert. Con said once that she liked coming to Florida because it was not a place she had ever visited with Aubrey; she missed him less there. My mother loved to hear the stories that Jim Newton told in the evenings, when they had dinner together at the Newtons' home on Estero Boulevard in Fort Myers Beach, at sunset. He talked about their sailing trips together, just before the war, just Jim and my father and mother, sailing through the Florida Keys and down Shark River and out to the Dry Tortugas. My father always handled a sailboat as if it were an airplane, my mother said, because he insisted that the principles of navigation were much the same in the air and on the sea. They sailed all day, and often at night, too. Each of the three friends would take turns at the tiller on the night watches, steering by the stars, just as my parents had navigated by the stars when they flew around the world together. They sailed in southern waters, on a boat that was itself named after a star, the *Aldebaran*. They were of the generation of navigators who placed their trust in celestial navigation, and aerodynamics, and one another.

On my desk, I have another photograph of my mother and my aunt, sitting on a park bench together, in Florida, in their eighties, my mother in a pink raincoat, Con in a blue sweater, each wearing her scallop shell pin.

In Florida, in winter, my mother walked on the beach every day, and every day politely asked whether Con would like to go with her. Con, every day, politely chose to stay. She did not walk as easily now as she had during those visits to Captiva, forty years earlier. One of my cousins told me that year that the trouble with her mother's feet was a very painful bunion.

Another speculated that perhaps her mother, after having been on her feet and active for so many years, simply wanted to sit down.

My mother excused her sister to me, in an undertone, one morning as we went out the door together onto the beach. "It is a great deal harder for her to walk long distances than it is for you and me. You see, she has always had such very small feet."

Con, however, read the daily newspapers avidly, and immediately figured out how to use both the microwave and the remote control on the television set in the condominium apartment. My mother, who claimed to have no skill whatsoever with appliances, said in beaming praise of her sister, "I don't know how you do it, dearie!" over and over again.

They both ate their meals sparingly, and politely. "Not too much, thank you!" they would murmur when dishes were passed or food was offered. "My, this is delicious," they would say. They brought with them to Florida the manners of Next Day Hill, and Casa Mañana, and Deacon Brown's Point. Outside their condominium window the easy waves of the Gulf of Mexico moved in and out so quietly that it was sometimes hard to believe it was really there.

19
Words

A word falls in the silence like a star
Searing the empty heavens with a scar
Of beautiful and solitary flight
Against the dark and speechless space of night

Anne Morrow Lindbergh, *The Unicorn and Other*
Poems (New York: Pantheon, 1956)

✳ ANNE and I walked together slowly along the same beach of the Gulf of Mexico in October of 1993, two months before Anne died. We had flown south for a brief time together, just the two of us, taking a vacation from the cancer by leaving town between two of her chemotherapy sessions, in honor of our birthday.

We were born on the same day, October 2, she in 1940, and I in 1945. We celebrated birthdays together for almost fifty years. When we were children in the old house in Darien, we would open presents piled in two separate armchairs in the living room, blow out candles on two separate cakes, and we would always receive at least one gift tangibly marking our lopsided twinship. There were white summer nightgowns, once, in our two separate sizes. The larger one had embroidered across the yoke in red script the French phrase "Bonne Nuit, Ma Chérie." The smaller one, inevitably, read "Bonne Nuit, Ma Petite," making me feel as if not only the garment but also the night itself was smaller for people my age. At the time this was a comforting idea.

Sometimes we got velvet dresses from our Grandma Bee, dark red or inky blue or even black, with lacy collars and thick sashes to be tied in bows at the back. Sometimes they were Lanz dresses, with silver buttons down the front and a cotton print of tiny hearts, or paper-doll Tyrolean children holding hands, across our chests and up and down the whole length of our arms. I loved these dresses, far more sumptuous than anything in my normal wardrobe. I felt both lucky and also smug about them, because I could wear our dressy twin-clothes twice as long as Anne did. First I would wear my own dress, for every single significant family occasion at home and for every Sunday grandmother dinner at Next Day Hill. Then, not immediately after I had grown too big for mine, but in a few years, I could wear Anne's, which she had outgrown. Her dress looked exactly like my old one, to everyone but me. To me, Anne's dresses were imbued with her personality, and when I wore them I wore her, too, affirming our double con-nection and our more-than-sisterhood every time I pulled the soft material over my head.

Anne told me that because I had been born on her birthday I was her property, and she even convinced me for a while that this unusual circumstance made me her slave, legally. She called me "Zombie," and sent me on missions around the house: to collect cookies, find misplaced books, spy on the brothers. Eventually I rebelled, but for a long time I was glad to serve. It was interesting to be a slave in Anne's world, a place where anything could happen.

I was not much like her, and I did not exactly feel possessive about my sister. Whether I belonged to her or not, she be-longed obviously and utterly to herself. All the same, I felt that I was a participant in her identity, with special knowledge of the two long blond braids, the fingernails scented with orange peels, the collection of tiny stuffed Steiff teddy bears she kept by her bedside, the stories she told when we took walks to-gether through the swamps and woods, peopling the marshes with colonies of creatures I could almost but not quite see behind the rotting stumps and deep inside the cattail tangles. There were "Red Buttons" and "Blue Buttons," small elflike wild people who were not necessarily nice, but who fought among themselves and were shy of passers-by. "Boggles," on the other hand, were aggressively clumsy, and knobby-kneed, and huge —sometimes they chased us down the roads, sometimes we chased them, shrieking victorious cries through the brambles, letting our legs catch thorns and bleed as we ran, scourging the wetlands with our voices.

On her bookshelves at home, Anne kept her diaries and her notebooks, lightweight journals bound in Florentine paper, red- or green- or butter-yellow-covered, with vined and curli- cued patterns like the wallpaper in old dollhouses. They were filled from first page to last with her looping up-and-down handwriting, and her poetry, and her drawings. I sneaked in to her room to read them once, when she was sixteen and out on a date, at night. I was eleven, and I read romance comics at my best friend's house a lot. I wanted to learn whether my sister had kissed anybody yet. I didn't find out. For one thing, she didn't write about her dates in the part of the diary that I read, and for another, I stopped reading when I found her drawings.

She did not sketch from nature, or draw princesses and butterflies, as I sometimes did. She rarely even drew horses, the favorite subject for so many other girls her age. Instead, she did line drawings in the style of James Thurber, usually of animals. The faces of the dogs, especially, suggested wisdom, a quizzical turn of mind, and probably the power of speech. Sometimes she drew thin, worried-looking men and women with musical instruments. I remember a bald man with a mus- tache, dodging behind a viola da gamba. He looked a lot like Corliss Lamont.

For a few years Anne had some white mice in her room, in

a cage with newspaper nests and toilet paper tube tunnels that they liked to chew on. On Sunday afternoons I could hear the sound of their scratchings and paper shreddings behind the long cool notes of my sister's flute. Anne practiced behind her closed door, which had its own shiny brass knocker on the outside, a birthday present from my mother's friend Dr. Atchley. I would pick up its little swinging horseshoe shape between my thumb and forefinger and let it drop three times to request entry. Sometimes my sister answered the knocking, and I was admitted. Sometimes she didn't, and I wasn't. Engraved upon the knocker in script, as on an old-fashioned calling card, was our family name for her, "Ansy."

People who knew Anne as an adult tend to talk about her abstractly, citing qualities like "beauty," "wit," "talent," "warmth," "brilliance." The words may be apt, but somehow they can't hold Anne at all. I don't think any words can. There was never a net she couldn't slip right through, never a way that generalities could tame or contain her specific and particular self. I can't describe my sister now that she has died any better than I could when she was living, but I can keep knowing her: hair, hands, eyes, laughter, her way of paddling a canoe at thirteen or of opening a screen door to let the dogs go out at fifty-two. I like knowing the way she pulled her winter hat over her ears, or the way she handed out the plate of candy to trick-or-treaters at Halloween. I like remembering what she looked like shoveling snow or starting a car or telling a joke or folding laundry. I love remembering that she used to keep a cup near the washer, for collecting loose change that fell out of the pockets of her family's clothing, and that she labeled it "Gift from the Sea." (Also, when our mother's first collection of diaries and letters appeared in print, called *Bring Me a Unicorn*, Anne and I were both struggling with work and small children, and she told me that her own memoir would be titled *Bring Me a Stiff Gin and Tonic*.)

It is true also that for all of Anne's life she seemed to me to be a person of enchantment, not in a fairytale, magic-wand-and-gossamer way, but as if she were a kind of female wizard, privy to charms and spells and ancient knowledge. She seemed not to belong entirely to the real world I lived in, but instead to another one that was her own, into which I had occasional privileged entry by right of birth.

I was forty-eight on our last birthday together, and Anne fifty-three. We walked out one October morning onto a quiet off-season beach, long and gray in the early light, with only a contemplative ripple disturbing the surface of the Gulf, and sand dunes and sea grass and pelicans all around us. A thousand tickling fiddler crabs scattered off in every direction.

We made up a toast to each other, that day, to our accumulation of 101 years, and to our families, and especially to our written words. We were proud of being writers, of living and working in the family tradition as professionals. And we knew that we carried that tradition on our backs, like book-bound turtles, as we moved through our writing lives. We knew that this was a complicated legacy.

"Write it down!" our mother had told us whenever we said something that particularly interested or touched her: write down that sharp insight, that funny story, that especially appealing turn of phrase. She taught us that any experience worth living through was worth writing about, but beyond this, she made us feel that the act of writing about it significantly affected the experience itself. I did not know whether writing enhanced an event, transforming it into something more important than it would have been had it gone unrecorded, or whether writing simply made it more real, like the testimony of an observant bystander who can confirm that *Yes, something has indeed happened here: I am a witness, and this is what I saw.*

For my mother, the relationship of writing and living was like the philosophical conundrum about the tree in the forest: If it falls to the ground, but nobody is around to hear it, does it make a sound? In my mother's philosophy the question would have been: Does the unwritten experience truly exist at all? Does it even matter?

My mother was as wedded to her identity as a writer as she was wedded to our father, and for that reason, perhaps, she gave herself little credit for being his co-pilot, navigator, and radio operator during the early flights around the world, or for being the first woman in America to earn a glider pilot's license. These were aspects of her life that had to do with her husband's career, not hers. She was a writer, first and foremost.

We children accepted the success of her 1955 book, *Gift from the Sea,* as a natural thing, and no more than her due. We began by being blasé about it, but soon became fiercely partisan. I remember how vicious my feelings were, in sixth grade, when Norman Vincent Peale's book *The Power of Positive Thinking* edged ahead of my mother's on the *New York Times* bestseller list.

Not long after this I developed an even more powerful hatred for the poet and critic John Ciardi, who had written what I considered a scurrilously nasty review of my mother's one volume of poetry, *The Unicorn and Other Poems,* in *The Saturday Review.* This book was published a year after *Gift from the Sea,* and like its predecessor, it is still in print and selling well forty years later. But in 1956, Ciardi was the newly assigned poetry editor of the *Review* and a distinguished poet himself. He disliked my mother's poems so much that he wrote several pages of contemptuous criticism, characterizing her work as "miserable," "slovenly," and "illiterate," and announcing to the *Review's* readers that "Mrs. Lindbergh has written an offensively bad book."

Ciardi's review drew an outraged response from her readers. The magazine's editor, Norman Cousins, felt compelled to publish a letter of his own, distancing himself from Ciardi's language and tone, while defending the poet's right to express his views.

I was not interested in the niceties of editorial policy, or in the rights of self-expression. I was not even interested in poetry, particularly, and at the time I had not read my mother's poems. When I finally did read them, some of the poems made me uncomfortable. They were often about death, and they had a formal quality that I did not recognize, and an emotional content that I did not understand. To read them made me feel acutely embarrassed, like the youngest person at a family funeral: overdressed and uncomprehending and hot around the neck.

I here; you there—
But under those eyes, space is all-where.

I alive; you dead—
But under those eyes, all-time is spread.

I alone—
But under those eyes, all things are joined;
All sorrow, and all beauty, and all spirit,
Are one.

Anne Morrow Lindbergh,
The Unicorn and Other Poems
(New York: Pantheon, 1956)

Much later in my life, to my humbled surprise, I rediscovered *The Unicorn*. I was comforted and sustained by poem after poem, heartened by my mother's imagery and craftsmanship, grateful for her voice. (I also became familiar with Ciardi's poetry and liked it very much, which annoyed me.)

At the time when John Ciardi wrote his review, I had no perspective as a reader at all. I didn't hate the critic for being wrong, I hated him for being *mean,* and I hated him with a purity of feeling that I usually reserved for people who hit their dogs, or slapped their children, or shot at the ducks in our marshes. In the episode of my mother's book review I found cruelty and injustice in an unexpected place, and I reacted accordingly.

I don't know that my mother ever knew how I felt. I knew, though, in the way that children know these things, however hard adults try to hide them, how she felt. She was devastated by the review, wrote very little verse after it appeared, and never published another volume of poetry. My sister told me that thirty years later, in the 1980s, when some of Anne's own poetry was about to be published, she announced the good news on a weekend visit to Connecticut, and saw our mother suddenly turn pale.

"Poetry? By Anne Lindbergh? Oh Ansy, but what about John Ciardi?"

My impression was that writing poetry was as painful for our mother as it was satisfying, anyway, even without the publication of *The Unicorn and Other Poems* and the disastrous Ciardi review that followed it. Generally, her poems have taken as their subjects the most profound events and feelings in her life: the death of a child or a parent, the distances in a marriage, the contemplation of old age. All of her written work, prose or poetry, tends to be confessional in nature, and while many of her poems are reflective or descriptive, most lay bare emotions that find their way only with great effort into written form. This is a kind of writing from which it is hard to recover, even when written in small doses. It never surprised me that she preferred the perspective provided by the personal essay, as in *Gift from the Sea,* and later by the collections of diaries and letters, with their long, thoughtful introductions.

In old age, sitting on the sofa before the fire, my mother rereads her own published diaries slowly, page after page. She will carefully mark special places in these diaries as she reads, sometimes leaving as many as fifty markers in one book. She will mark her place, or her places, with scraps of paper, envelopes, napkins, pieces of ribbon, whatever comes to hand. Since she does not mark the pages in any other way, not with pencil, pen, or spoken comment, I cannot tell what it is that these markers denote. I don't feel that it is my business to ask, either. If she wants to tell me, if she remembers long enough, she will do so, unsolicited. In the meantime, what she finds in her diaries is hers alone, as it was when she wrote it down in the first place.

She does not read her poems at all, and does not let me read them to her.

"Stop!" she said, holding up her hand as forcefully as if holding back a line of traffic, when I tried to read aloud the one called "No Angels" in her presence. The gesture was unmistakable. It came from an impulse much fiercer than modesty, and a feeling more honest than coy self-deprecation. I stopped. I know better than to confront a writer with her own words when she doesn't want to be confronted. This can be a very specialized form of assault.

My father believed that my mother was not only a great writer, but also a Great Writer, one of the most important writers of the twentieth century. He said this to us in different ways, many different times, but our mother was never happy about it.

"Nonsense, Charles!" she would tell him, irritated rather

than flattered by the sloppy enormity of his praise. She liked to refer to her writing as her "craft," and resisted the aggrandizement of her efforts with the same self-denying vehemence with which she refused to put butter on her baked potato, or to wear the color green. Writing for my mother was not only a kind of breathing, her respiratory system for experience, but was also a form of meditation, even a secular religion. Writing was worth suffering over, she taught us. Writing was worth both the effort and the emotion she so fully gave to it. Writing was worth pursuing, in one form or another, even after the most destructive attacks by critics. But to brag about being "good at it," to accept too seriously the praises and honors offered by others, this would have been a kind of sacrilege.

20
Father

✳ WHEN my father died in Hawaii, in August of
1974, it took me a long time to believe he was really dead. I
knew that he was dying that summer, just as I knew twenty
years later, in the beginning of a gray winter, that my sister was
dying, too. But it seemed impossible that either one of them
would actually die. Maybe they didn't believe it, either. Maybe
none of us, ever, really does believe in our own death. My
father only days before his death told my brother Scott that he
thought he had an "outside chance" of beating the lymphatic
cancer that had invaded his body so completely that the doctors could not treat it anymore; my sister told me ten days
before she died that she had figured out how to take her tubes
and medications with her when she camped with her husband,
next spring, in the little cabin they were building on a piece of
land in northern Vermont.

My father's was the first profoundly important death of my
life, and I did not know at the time how fortunate he was in
his passing. He had little pain, according to both my mother's
reports and his own, and he was able to explore the weaknesses
and debilitations of his body with an intact and penetrating
mind. I had thought he would die harder. I had feared that
frustration over the weakness in his body would betray him

into helpless anger and hopeless dependency, both unbearable for me to witness.

I should have known better. Yes, there was some anger and frustration in my father at times, but more often a great energy, and a spirit of adventure about his own dying that I should have expected. It was characteristic of him that he was unfailingly alert during his last months and weeks, if not always easy to be with; if often cantankerous; if sometimes pathetically vulnerable in appearance. Even when I found his appearance most pathetic, though, he surprised me with his resilience and stamina. I knew he was a strong person, but I had not known he was strong in this way.

As is so often true, I discovered that I had the most to fear not from the condition of my dying father, but from my own inner condition. Wavering, exhausted, pregnant with my second child, my emotions seesawing with each piece of news, I traveled with my mother and my siblings into my father's death. I recorded the journey in my diary, sometimes cryptically in a few sentences, sometimes at brooding length over several pages, writing my thoughts and feelings down as my mother had taught me to do, all the way to the end.

6/24/74 Peacham, Vermont

Father is working hard on his various manuscripts. His legs are bony, but his head is just the same, and his eyes, and his energy. But he looks awful in a hospital gown, and so thin. But his head is extraordinary, always. "Indomitable!" the doctor said of him to Mother. I encouraged her, all weekend, told her he could turn all that energy into writing, and how well he was adapting to illness, and how strong he was, and how wonderful to see him adapt to illness—such a surprise that he is not rejecting it! Another resource of character.

He never stops amazing me. Just when I think I know what he's like, he behaves in a whole new way. I never thought he would admit illness, but he's sort of exploring it. I was "supporting" and "warm" and full of good cheer, and then when I got home to Peacham I began to cry, and am finding it hard to stop. My father being thin in a hospital gown seems like the saddest thing in the world . . .

7/27/74 Saturday, Darien

A heavy, sunless day. The cove is calm, with herons on the island and Canada geese in the reeds by Mother's little inlet. Mother and I both woke in the night—about 3 a.m.—and talked for an hour on her bed. We each cried a little, but as she said it is "healing." You are overcome, you cry, and it washes something out of you so you can start again. She claims I help her by being here, but I am not sure. I keep trying to press things of myself upon her—a nice picture of me with Molly [our dog] and the littlest lamb; a water-color sketch I did in North Haven (the islands and the Camden Hills). Vanity? Or trying to tell her I am here, and would give her everything? She goes in to Father [at Columbia Presbyterian Hospital in New York City] today. I'll go tomorrow, after resting some, if I can.

I am afraid to go—what will it be like? Will I break down?—But I'm anxious to be there just to give him a hug or a kiss, or tell him somehow how much I love him . . . I don't want to be soggy or burdensome in my feelings . . . I don't want to bother him . . .

The phone rings all day. How Mother can stand it I can't imagine. The head nun at the monastery she visits in upstate Connecticut suggests that Mother baptize him ("It's quite simple, really, just a little water . . ."). Connie Fulenwider calls twice to say that Doc [Dr. John Rosen, who treated my Uncle Dwight] is all set to drive up here and iron out any psychological problems (of Mother's) during these weeks, Barbara and Jon call to say that [their son] Lars (14 now, I think) is in Connecticut with [Mother's friends] the

Chamberlains—couldn't he go in and cheer Father up? I envision a parade—Lars and Dr. Rosen and The Mother Superior all together descending on the Intensive Care unit of Columbia Presbyterian. People are so unfailingly absurd. At the end of the evening Mother and I were suddenly laughing to the point of tears in the kitchen, when finally the last of the telephoners had hung up.

7/28/74 Sunday

It was wonderful to see him. I felt all day, before we went in, that same dread I used to feel on days when I knew I was going to Dr. Shoup's for a shot—would I disgrace myself? How many hours before the moment of confrontation? What would happen? What chasms of feeling were waiting for me?

But he put his hand up on the guard-rail and said sleepily how good it was to see me, and I felt so happy to be there. I held his hand for 45 minutes, and he talked and rested, and talked again, asking about the baby-to-be, and Lizzie, and Richard [Brown, my first husband], and the cats (he always wants to know how many cats we have—I guess because we once had 9), telling me I had to have 3 children ("with 2 you don't replace yourself") . . . He talked about how he hated air conditioners and what a damn nuisance his shingles were (bothering him again now).

But he was so much himself. Uncomplaining and down-to-earth and direct and vital. Having that time with him was a gift I'll never lose, and his strength is another. I love him and love him and love him.

I remember looking down at the table beside the hospital bed and seeing a blue airmail pad, one of his notepads. I saw that written on the pad in pencil in my father's handwriting were these words: "I know there is an infinity outside ourselves. I wonder now if there is an infinity within, as well?" I

have never seen this written again, in any of his papers, but I
have thought about it often since that day.

8/7/74 Wednesday

*We left Darien to come back here two days after I visited Father.
Ansy arrived with her family and Scott was about to come. It
seemed too crowded with people and feelings, too much for Mother
to have so many of us, and right that the European ones [Scott and
Anne], who have had so little of Father lately, should be there. It
should, I suppose, have seemed melodramatic and final as we drove
away, but in fact we were happy to be going home. Father is
somehow better. Scott went to see him, and there was a complete
reconciliation. Scott goes in every day or so, and they talk, and
amazingly, Father is feeling much better, is out of Intensive Care
and sitting up in a chair, reading, and badgering Mother to work
on her manuscript instead of visiting him. Ansy went in several
times, and saw him change. I suppose it won't last, but he is
extraordinary—the doctors are all very surprised at his rallying.
We are granted a lull, in this nightmare.*

8/12/74 Monday, Peacham

*We are very far away, here, from what is happening to my
parents. An oasis for Ansy and me, because Father isn't dramati-
cally worse just now, and here it's been beautiful weather and happy
days. . . . We swim at the lake, pick cherries and make pies, sit out
under the maple trees or on the porch. We have been canoeing, and
for dinner at Rabbit Hill, and for walks to see the Jones' new colt
or way down the road towards Stevenson's. Julien [Anne's first
husband] plays the piano, Charles [their son] keeps catching frogs,
the girls run in and out with no clothes on, stick their tongues out
at one another, share noisy baths. . . .*

*It's as if he had gone on one of his trips, that kind of absence.
But every so often it hits me. Mother planning what to do if he wants*

*to come home—"The doctors say it will have to be professional
—a hospital bed, round-the-clock-nurses, a doctor very near, a
commode. . . ." I fight the visions, selfishly. And then the desolate
certainty that nothing has changed. If he's home it won't be for long.*

8/17/74 Saturday, North Haven, Maine

They are going to Maui.

*Mother called last night, here, to say that was what he wanted
to do. Tonight he called us himself, spoke with Ansy and me.
Slow, tired, but unmistakably him. He said his condition was "very
serious," and that he wasn't afraid of death. Given a choice, he said,
he'd say no to it, but since he had no choice he wasn't apprehensive.
And even though the doctors made a fuss at his wanting to leave
the hospital, he said it was a "philosophical decision." I sent him a
hug and he sent one back, and lots of love. I said it was wonderful
for us, his children, to see "how he faced this," and he said in a
typically testy fashion that it wasn't a question of "facing" anything.
He wasn't worried about it, but he'd been in the N.Y. hospital long
enough. Dr. Howell has found him a cottage to rent near the Hana
hospital. Jon and Scott will fly out with him and Mother, and Land
will meet them in Honolulu. They have a block of seats on United.*

*Julien was saying it was legendary—the three sons taking the
father back to the homeland—and it is, mythical even. I am so
grateful for Father's lack of sentimentality, his vastness and his
practicality at all times. "Dans les détails il a toujours bon goût,"
said Julien tonight. Not only that, but he is taking control of his life,
taking it out of the hands of the doctors and away from the anxious-
ness of his children, out of the realm of hovering and deceit (he
knows how slim his chances are. For the last few days he's been
finishing up details—his will, manuscripts for Harcourt Brace, lists
for Mother—I always thought he wasn't ready for death, but in his
own way he's readier than anybody. He told Mother that he'd much*

rather be dead than spend his life in a hospital, and that it was a kind of adventure) and into a peaceful place.

"It is rather convenient," Mother said wearily (and I think it is again his energy, even now, that wears on her as much as anything), "to die where you want to be buried." I am sure he has thought of that, too. Dr. Atchley says all he needs is oxygen, there's nothing else they can give him that will make any difference. I guess the oxygen makes him more comfortable . . . I love to think of him flying to Maui. I hope he gets there.

8/24/74 Peacham

He did, of course. Safely and comfortably flew to Maui with Mother and all the brothers, counter to the doctors' warnings and predictions—how delighted he must have been at confounding them! They refused even to give him a certificate to leave the hospital and fly, but Sam Pryor [an old Pan Am friend] got the United Airlines doctor to do it—and he has been in Maui a week with very little change in his condition. (Scott called on his way home from Hawaii back to France and [his wife] Alika, who must be sorely tried, left for 3 weeks with 40 monkeys.) Apparently he is entering into preparations for the future with great gusto: arranging with carpenters and so forth about a coffin, and having the grave dug ahead of time—doing everything himself (calling people and having them come to the cottage, where he's in bed but has a phone) so that nothing is left unarranged.

He was bound to be orderly about it, I knew that. Of course he made it his business to monitor the grave-digging arrangements—he wanted a traditional Hawaiian grave, wide and deep and full of stones—and he talked with the man in charge of digging it, Tevi Kahaleuahi, who assured him that the job would be so well done that he, Tevi, would be tempted to

jump right in with my father when the time came. He talked
over possible hymns for his funeral, too, and liked having my
mother sing hymns to him during his last few days, auditioning
them, as it were. "That one's too corny," he told her once,
emphatically, when she thought he was almost asleep.

*Scott says he seems to be having quite a good time. But also that
he's bullying Mother, which is very painful for her. Getting into those
speeches that go "I told you over and over and over again . . ." and
making odd requests. He still thinks there is a chance he'll pull
through this, Scott says, but he doesn't want to be unprepared. . . .
Mother called when Ansy and I were out the other day, to try to get
hold of a Hudson Bay blanket that he wants to be buried in. Scott
says there was a long discussion among all the men about whether
he should have a cow hide in with him too.*

*I am in an odd state of separateness, and can't do anything but
laugh. How typical of him to turn obnoxious, just when we were all
getting so sentimental. . . .*

The day my father died, I knew that it had happened, or
thought I did, before anyone ever told me so. I was driving
home from a grocery store in Danville, Vermont, late in August,
and all at once there was a brightening in the sky above and in
front of me, and a thinning intensity of light amid the cloud
formations to the south and west. I felt a quality of atmospheric
ease, both meteorological and emotional, and a sudden relief
from the minute-by-minute anxiety I had experienced during
the past weeks. I thought immediately that this must be the
day of my father's death, and almost as immediately dismissed
the premonition. At this point, I told myself severely, any day
at all could be the day of my father's death. Shortly after I got
home, though, Land called from Hawaii.

August 26, 1974   Monday

Father died at 7:15 this morning, Maui time—"very peacefully,"
after a full night's sleep under some sedation. Last night he ap-
parently had trouble breathing, and asked for more oxygen, and
for sedation to make his body relax. "I'm not afraid," is what Land
told me he said, "but my body is afraid," and so it was making
the oxygen harder to take, or something. He told them between
spells of breathing trouble that he had just then felt very close
to death several times and that it did not bother him. He kept them
in touch with how he was feeling (much better with the oxygen)
until he fell asleep, and this morning he was still asleep and
breathing "shallowly" when the doctor came to take him to the
hospital . . . and then I guess he breathed less and less, and the
doctor saw what was happening, and didn't try to move him, and
then he died.

Land said it was really quite beautiful, and not painful at all—
no struggle, even the short period of breathing trouble didn't seem
to panic or change Father. I am so proud of him for not changing,
for getting away clean, and being himself the whole time. For not
having to be in a hospital, for not deteriorating or ranting or raving
or raging. It changes the whole idea of death for me, makes it
reasonable, quiet.

The doctor had insisted to the family the night before that
with this new breathing trouble, my father would have to be
transported to the local hospital in the morning, something he
had hoped to avoid, and did. By the time the ambulance arrived in the morning he was in a coma, close to death, breathing less and less. Dr. Howell, an old friend, knew enough about
both medicine and friendship not to interfere.

Several times, when someone I love has died, I have felt a
kind of elation at the news, an emotion I have rarely shared
with other people because it shocks me to feel it. I used to

think this feeling must be what Anne and I called "Victim's High," the elevated, unreal rush of excitement and significance that follows terrible news or terrible diagnosis, a heightened sense of being alive in the midst of great peril, or great personal loss.

Everyone wants everyone else to feel all right. Mother wanted to tell Ansy (through me, since a Maui–France call would be difficult if not impossible) how much Father liked talking to her on Sunday (Ansy called Maui before flying back to France) and then in the same breath she assured me that it was wonderful I didn't talk to him when I called the other day, to tell them the Hudson Bay blanket had been sent. (I left a message with the nurse, because I wasn't sure what she meant when she said my mother was "out" but my father was "up," and I didn't think I had enough to say to make it worth his exertion—also ancient fear of his wrath at unnecessary long distance calls. "The blanket? Is that what you called about? Reeve!" etc. . . .)

She said how wonderful to have spared him that much breath, and that he got the message and was terribly pleased, and not at all hurt that I hadn't spoken to him (didn't even know I was on the phone when I called). So Ansy was good to talk to Father and I was good not to—How delicious Mother is at all times!

He was joking with them about the service yesterday afternoon. Mother kept singing psalms, and he teased her, and was happy.

Ansy had only been home a few days when I called. "Oh, Reeve!" she said, she so tired and I so shaky and even exhilarated by that sense of Father's beautiful escape. But for Ansy all the thoughts about it ("very peaceful," "no pain," "Land said it was much more acceptable than he expected") are just the Emperor's New Clothes.

"I don't want to think," she said, and promised to call Scott right

away, and hung up. I keep throwing silver linings at her, and all she
wants are the facts. Poor Ansy!

I didn't feel like crying until CBS had a news brief about him—
how did they find out so fast?—a short film on his life, ending with
a conservation speech from last September. (The hardest thing to
take.) Richard and I have known him so well just lately, and to hear
his voice was a shock and dissolved my bravery. I am so familiar
with his aspect of the last few years, and there it all was in front of
me for a second, and then Roger Mudd or someone summing up—
"Charles Lindbergh, dead at 72." And that was it. Slam. They take
him so far away.

But the truth is that my father took himself away, dying
exactly as he had wanted to do, in quietness, in a place he
loved, with his family all around him, and with that immensity
of waters, the Pacific Ocean, bearing witness to his fading
heartbeat at the last.

My father has been dead for almost a quarter of a century now,
but I still miss him, and I expect I always will. Still, whenever
I want to find him again, I travel to Minnesota to visit his
boyhood home, the Lindbergh house and farm in Little Falls. I
do this even though the Lindbergh home in Little Falls is an
odd place for me to look for my father. For more than seventy
years it has belonged to the state of Minnesota and not to my
family at all. Furthermore, the Lindbergh family life that took
place there, day to day, has nothing to do with my childhood
or my adult life, and dates back to the years before 1920, a
time even more distant to my family than the flight of the *Spirit
of St. Louis.*

Like the aircraft hanging in the great gallery of the Smithsonian Air and Space Museum, the house in Little Falls seems

an artifact of our family's pioneer days, a vestige of such unfamiliar and ancient times that to present-day Lindbergh children, and grandchildren, and great-grandchildren, it might just as well be a covered wagon.

Why does this place speak so strongly to me? I never went to Little Falls with my father, and was not even fully aware of how much it meant to him until a year or two before his death. He occasionally talked about, but never personally introduced me to, the old house on the bank of the upper Mississippi, with its wood-burning cook stove and its glassed-in china cabinets and its steep stairs. He mentioned once or twice in passing, but never showed me directly, the wide, screened porch overlooking the riverbank where as a boy he kept a cot and blankets, summer and winter, because whenever he got the chance, he liked to sleep at least halfway outdoors. If I close my eyes today I can see him there, on his cot, stretching out to his full length in contentment, a young, long, lean boy, on a farm by a river, in 1918, with his dog, Wahgoosh, curled up at his feet.

Now that I know the house and farm, and have been there many times, I think I know the boy and his dog, too, breathing quietly in each other's presence, eyes open, listening for a long time in the dark before sleep comes over either one of them, hearing together the night sounds of the farm, and the comforting creak and settle of the house beside them, and the wet, whispered running of the river, the young, long, lean Mississippi River, in the headlong inevitable rush of its own Minnesota beginnings, running by. I like knowing that my father slept with the Mississippi River running right by him where he lay, on its way from the swimming holes and berry bushes of Little Falls to a destiny of faraway grandeurs and immensities, flowing first to Minneapolis, and then to Dubuque, and Hannibal, and St. Louis, and Memphis, and Baton Rouge, and finally all the way out to spill itself completely into the Gulf of Mexico.

My father, too, had come such a long way from his beginnings that it took time to reestablish him in my imagination here, in Minnesota, in his early home. It was a hard task, but a familiar one, to reclaim him from his own history and make him mine. This effort in itself causes one of the strangest interminglings I have come to know as the child of famous parents: the give-and-take between public impression and private memory, each informing, educating, correcting, and ultimately humanizing the other, over time. It is an important effort, however odd or uncomfortable it sometimes feels. I have learned that by pursuing my own history consistently, pursuing it with compassion and without fear, I will discover over and over again that the people I love best can never be lost to me, after all.

The Minnesota Historical Society guides who lead the tours through what is now the Lindbergh Home and Historical Site have by now pointed out many things to me that my father never did. These guides seem warmly enthusiastic about this house, and speak with a kind of nostalgic, affectionate familiarity of the family whose home it once was. Many of them are women, people who have retired from other jobs in nearby towns, and they seem to me remarkably well versed both in the history of the region and that of my family. In fact, when I first came to Little Falls, I was embarrassed to discover how much more most Minnesota natives knew about my ancestors than I did. With well-chosen words and lilting voices, here and there even a trace of a Scandinavian accent—so many Minnesotans, like my father, are descended from the Swedes and Norwegians and Danes who settled this part of the country a century ago—they guided me through the house room by room, and I felt a double identity as I followed the tour: I was a relative of the house, I had connections with these rooms, these books, these beds, this china. Surely I should remember something here, and feel some sense of recognition? At the same time I was just one more person in the parade of thousands of visitors who come through every year between May and October, the season when the Lindbergh Home and Historical Site are both open to the public.

I had a sense of history here, but I should have had more personal feelings, I thought. I had been hearing the stories about the farm in Little Falls quite recently, most often in the late 1960s and early 1970s, when my father was visiting his boyhood home often, first to help with historical research and then to make a speech at the dedication of the small museum built in 1972, just down the road from the old house. The house and 110-acre farm were originally established as a state park by the Minnesota legislature in 1931, when the property was given to the state in memory of my grandfather, C.A. Lindbergh, by his heirs: Evangeline, my father, his half-sister Eva, and the two children of his half-sister Lillian, who had died as a young woman.

At the time of the gift the house was in poor repair, partly because it had been empty since 1920, when my father and his mother left the farm, but also because of damage caused by souvenir seekers after my father's flight to Paris in 1927. Over time, both the exterior and interior were restored, and many original family furnishings were collected and returned, until by 1969 a major renovation project was under way, the complete restoration of the home as it had been during the time my father lived there.

I did not even know, until my father began to be so busy about it in the 1960s, that the old farm still existed, not just a memory but a real place that I could someday visit. All the stories my father told about the farm during my earlier childhood were so deeply embedded in the past that there seemed no possibility of a present-day connection. I knew only that before I was born, before the Second World War, before the kidnapping, before the flight to Paris, before the *First* World War, before my father had an airplane to fly or even a car to drive, he was a boy on a farm in Minnesota. I understood that this part of his life took place long, long before my time, in the era that my sister and I called "The Olden Days." I felt that it was far out of my reach geographically, too, set in a part of the country known to my New England mind as "Way out West."

I do remember my father telling us how cold the winters were in central Minnesota when he was a boy, how deep and quiet and all-encompassing the snows. I remember hearing about the lilac and honeysuckle bushes his mother planted along the road in front of her house, and how good the sweet corn tasted that grew in Morrison County in the summer, better than anywhere else in the world.

I visited the house in Minnesota for the first time in the summer of 1975, a year after my father's death. My husband and I were driving back across the country after a visit with our two young daughters to my brother Land in Montana. I missed my father, and wanted very much to seek out the house and farm in Little Falls that year, hoping I would find a reminder of him there, and that it would give me comfort in some way.

There was a comforting feeling about the old house, certainly, with its gray clapboard frame and red roof, in a wooded setting near the river. When we walked up the wooden steps and in the front door there was a familiarity, too, to the heavy frame and darkly polished wood of the sofa in the living room, a recognizable gleam in the sturdy, glassed-in bookcases, and a remembered darkness in the carpets that absorbed the noise of our footsteps across the living room floor. The house in Minnesota, in fact, reminded me immediately of the house in Detroit, and of Farmor and Uncle. I was not surprised to learn that much of the furniture from my grandmother's home had been sent to the farm in Minnesota after her death. None of it, though, reminded me of my father as I knew him.

I did not find any trace of him in the dining room, with its table set neatly with china and dishes "used by Charles and his mother," as the guide pointed out. I liked the idea of his sleeping on the porch, but could not yet see him on the cot there, and I did not find him in the upstairs bedroom where his books and toys were carefully displayed: stories of boys' adventures on the high seas, or desert islands, or the western plains; tin soldiers and cannons, a collection of arrowheads and stones, a turtle shell. I did not find him in the voluminous, high-ceilinged basement, the tidiest basement I've ever seen, with its octopus of pipes and ducts for plumbing and heating, and its reminders of the two winters my father spent actually running the farm, during the First World War. Never a successful high school student and always preoccupied by the farm, he was delighted to learn that by growing food for the nation during wartime he could receive full academic credit, without attending high school at all. He left school immediately, and returned only to receive his diploma in 1918.

In the dark and spacious neatness of my father's basement, I saw an old saddle that had belonged to his own father, along with a motorcycle he himself had used in his teens and early twenties. I loved the brooder boxes he had made to house his baby chicks, just as I had loved coming upon the small round duck pond he had built of poured concrete in a fenced-in area he made for waterfowl, to the southwest of the house. He had called it "Moo Pond," and had scratched both the date of its construction and the name of his dog, Wahgoosh, in its concrete rim. I admired the well he had dug by hand the winter of 1918, in the northwest corner of the basement, when he was sixteen years old, and the gasoline engine, pump, and pressure tank which he had installed at the same time.

I nodded appreciation at everything I saw, and answered the guide's gentle questioning—yes, this was just the way I would have imagined it, no, the house did not particularly remind me of my life with my father, though it tallied with the stories he had told me about his boyhood. On I strolled, interested and detached. I was completely unprepared for what happened to me next, in the kitchen.

I came around a corner behind the guide, and caught a glimpse of a heavy black cast-iron frying pan, sitting empty on one burner of the old cook stove. Immediately, unmistakably, without any warning at all, my father was there with me in the room. His presence was a blow that almost doubled me over, in sharp recognition and sharper grief. I could see him, I could hear him. Not in Minnesota, but at home in Darien, with an identical pan in our own kitchen. He was at the stove, cooking something smelly—herring, probably, with onions and potatoes—bending over the sticky mess, concentrating hard, then turning around and grinning at me, mischievous and self-satisfied and hungry, in his blue nylon shirt and khaki trousers, and his desert boots.

"Nothing holds the heat like a black-iron pan!" my father pointed out to me, as he had done so many times before. He was ebullient, gesturing with the spatula. His one lock of white hair was falling loosely across the bald spot on top of his head, and I knew that his right hand would soon go into the pocket of his khaki chinos and come out with the black Ace comb. Then everything came together all at once: faraway history, Minnesota childhood, famous flight, Darien household, lectures, kippered herring, and all. He was here. I had found him. I burst into tears.

It took me a while to stop crying, to the discomfort of my

family and the consoling murmurs of the Lindbergh Home
guide. I am not discreet in distress—I weep noisily, with puffy
eyes, red blotches on my face, and sniffling—but when it was
over the whole atmosphere had changed. The guide told me
about her meetings with my father during his recent visits to
the farm, and about her own life in Little Falls. She took me to
see the car my father had left in Little Falls on one of his visits,
when he had driven west to the farm but had then been called
away suddenly, flying out of Minneapolis and leaving the car
behind. Later, he wrote to the Historical Society to tell them he
had decided to give them the vehicle, if they had any use for
it. I was amused to see our old Volkswagen, the one I had
learned to drive in, with a dent still in the left front fender
where I'd run into the stone wall at the curve of our driveway.

What amused me about the car when I saw it in Little Falls
was that it had not been used around the farm, as my father
suggested, but instead had been placed reverently on display,
in the company of another automobile my father had bought,
in 1916. This one was a Saxon Six, purchased for a trip to
California with his mother, from Farrow's Garage in Little Falls.
It has now been restored meticulously by the Minnesota National Guard, and is still occasionally driven in town parades.
(In 1997, during the seventieth anniversary celebration of the
flight to Paris, three of his great-grandchildren rode in it.)

The Saxon looked to me like a bona fide antique, fresh
with green paint and bright polish and gleaming brass. The
Volkswagen, on the other hand, had the drab, nondescript
aspect and color my father always favored during my childhood, and it astonished me that the Historical Society had
carefully draped my father's travel gear—sleeping bag, air mattress, plastic water jug, and sardine cans—along the passenger
seat and down the interior, I suppose so that people could see
how Charles Lindbergh habitually traveled during the years

following his flight. I wanted to point out that for authenticity they really needed one of his shoes, unlaced and opened wide to pillow his head, but I kept quiet because by that time I felt I had already caused enough commotion for one visit.

I have learned over the course of many subsequent visits to Little Falls that this is the best place for me to come if I want to understand my father and our family and even myself. Some of the most difficult things in our history have begun to make sense to me in Minnesota, and some of the most painful ones have begun to heal.

It was in Little Falls that I first heard my father's voice on tape in the Des Moines speech of 1941. His tone had a more nasal twang in it than I remembered from my years with him, and he was telling the world that one of the greatest dangers to pre–World War II America was the influence of Jews in prominent public positions.

It was not the first time I had come across this speech but it was the first time I had heard it spoken in my father's own voice. I was again transfixed and horrified, again ablaze with shame and fury—"Not you!" I cried out silently to myself, and to him—"No! You never said such things! You raised your children never to say, never even to *think,* such things—this must be somebody else talking. It can't be you!" I felt a global anguish—the horror of the Holocaust, the words of my own father ignoring the horror, but surely not condoning the horror, surely not dismissing, or diminishing it, surely not. But I also felt a piercingly personal rage, and if I could have written it down it would have looked like this: *"How could you do this to Mother? How could you leave her with this? Just die, and leave her alone, to answer the charges this speech forever invites? Why didn't you leave instructions, Father? Why didn't you tell us what to do about these words you left behind, on tape, before I was born, with this reputation that does not fit my experience of you? Did you think it was enough to ignore the accusers, to say briefly, tight-lipped, 'I'm not anti-Semitic!' and ask us with your own silence to do nothing at all, to say nothing at all, forever? Do you know how hard that is? Do you know what you have asked of us? Do you have any idea what it feels like to be someone who loved you, and is left with this? How could you have done this to us? How could you have done this to me?"*

There was no question in my mind about what my father was saying, or its implications. What I really wanted to know was, what did he *think* he was saying? Did he really believe that he was simply, dispassionately "stating the facts," as he later persistently claimed, without understanding that the very framework of the statement reverberated with anti-Semitic resonance? And if he really believed what he believed, and really did not understand what he did not understand, was that in itself not a form, however innocent he might think it, of anti-Semitism? Was there, in fact, such a thing as innocent, unconscious anti-Semitism? Was it prevalent before the war, and did the Holocaust forever criminalize an attitude that was previously acceptable and widespread among the non-Jewish population of this country and others? And was it this "innocence" or "unconsciousness" that I heard in my father's speech? Or was I simply playing with semantics and denying the obvious?

Certainly, I had seen, and read, what I considered by the standards of my generation to be clear evidence of racism, however he might deny any such thing, in some of my father's writings of the same period—most of which, again, I did not encounter until after his death.

What I wanted to know most of all, when I heard the Des Moines speech on tape in Minnesota, was this: How could someone who spoke the words my father did in 1941, never repudiating or amending them for the rest of his life, how did such a person then raise children who, by his instruction and his example, day after day and year after year, had learned from him—not simply from our mother, but from him too—that such words were repellent and unspeakable? How could that happen, and what did it mean, not just for my own family, but for others? And there are, indeed, many others who struggle as I do with the words spoken and written by past generations, words left by the very people whom they have most loved and respected, words they cannot accept.

I was born after the war, and I know that there are many things I will never understand about my family history, and the history of the era, many things I cannot understand about the ways that words and philosophies alter and are re-interpreted over time. I know, too, that there is great and dangerous arrogance in passing judgment upon our parents, and I wonder, when we do so, whether we invite our children, in turn, to pass judgment upon us. But the questions remain, as the words do. They burn themselves into us, individual by individual, family by family, generation after generation. I think we ourselves cannot truthfully answer the questions we would ask the generation that has come before us. But I am beginning to believe that we can at least create, with the honest anguish of our asking, a gift that may hearten the generation to come.

I can't answer the questions I wanted to ask my father when I first visited his home in Minnesota, but I have come back again and again, carrying with me what I already knew of him, bringing away what I did not.

I know that my father was a good boy, growing up in Minnesota, and that he grew into a good man. He was a man who continued to grow, along with his own century, through aviation and technology and war and peace and family life, and love. When he said late in life, "If I had to choose, I'd rather have birds than airplanes," he did not believe that he really had to choose, or that the world really had to choose, but he knew that there was much work ahead for him, and for us all, if birds and airplanes were to co-exist in harmony far into the technological future.

He was a man who loved his family and who loved his country, too, in a way that seems old-fashioned to many people now, but that comes naturally enough to those who know the country very well from earliest childhood, with a physical as well as an emotional understanding. When his life became more complicated than he ever had wished it or expected it to be, he was able to reach back to that understanding, to an affection for the earth he had known and experienced in his childhood, combined with a never-ending fascination for the land he had flown over as a young pilot, and the world he came to know internationally, as an older pilot. This love for the living earth, and for life itself, was his earliest strength, second only to his association with my mother in its intensity, and strong enough that it sustained him all the way through the very last days of his life.

I have never gotten over my original feeling that in Minnesota, all the elements in my father are finally brought together, and that here, if I can only pay close enough attention, he will be fully restored to me, time and time again. Everything is there: the childhood and the farm, the birds and the airplanes, the marriage, the war, the family, the conservation work, and the final days in Maui. Here, ever more open to my understanding as I make room to accommodate them, are gathered in one place both the simple truths and the complicated ones, each well grounded in the real life of a boy in the early 1900s, in the work and the rhythms of a farm, and in the long, strong running of a great American river, always growing wider, and flowing deeper, as it finds its way from town to town and farm to farm, always moving steadily toward the ocean.

21
Only a Suggestion

✳ H E taught her to fly when they were both still in their twenties, and he used to say that she was as good a pilot as he was, maybe better. Standing with me in the parking lot of a small airport in Vermont, in her sixties, she could easily pick out his rented plane from among a half dozen others in the air. They all looked exactly the same to me, and they were all circling the area similarly, waiting to land. How could she be sure which one of them was his, I asked.

"It's the way he wiggles his wings," she said, as if that explained everything, and perhaps it did.

I was reminded of that day twenty years later, in Washington, D.C., in the autumn of 1993, when my mother and I visited the Smithsonian Air and Space Museum, to see the *Spirit of St. Louis* and the *Tingmissartoq*, the Lockheed Sirius seaplane in which my parents had flown together in the 1930s. My mother had come to Washington the night before to receive an award presented at the Library of Congress by the Women in Aviation and Aerospace organization. In the morning, she wanted to see the airplanes.

She did not talk about the past at all on our flight to Washington, or during the evening's event. When we visited the museum the next day, she was content to walk around with friends and to look at the planes without comment: my father's *Spirit,* suspended from the vast central ceiling of the museum, in the company of the Wright Brothers' first Kitty Hawk experiment and other lightweight early aircraft, all so sharply in contrast to the dominating mass of NASA rockets nearby. We went upstairs and stood by the Sirius, now mounted on a broad balcony at second-floor level, not far from Amelia Earhart's airplane, surrounded by period photographs and explanatory text.

I read the words and looked at the old, familiar photographs of my parents, young and smiling in their flying suits. She used to complain to her daughters that *his* flying suit accentuated his tallness and slimness, while *hers,* in the photographs, seemed at the same time to diminish her height and to inflate her width, making her look like a little balloon with legs. Looking at the photographs once again, in Washington, I disagreed with her. A small and very happy young woman dressed in a large and cumbersome outfit smiled out at the world. To me she did not look inflated, like a balloon, but emergent, like a butterfly, perhaps somewhat hampered by her cocoon, but certainly more than ready to take to the air.

What struck me most when I looked at the pictures this time, and when I looked at the plane, was the height of the airplane, especially the vertical distance between the pontoons and the cockpits. It would have been a real stretch even for my father to get into this airplane, and he was over six feet tall. How could my mother, flying suit or no flying suit, have climbed into that aircraft at all?

I marveled aloud to my mother at the gymnastics that must have been required of her every time she got in or out of the Sirius. How did she do it? There were a few footholds or handgrips on the aircraft that I could see from where I was standing, but they seemed inadequate. Did my father hoist her up? My mother put her hand on my arm, and smiled.

"But he made me a little ladder, of course."

Of course.

My parents flew together all over the world, and were joined in marriage for close to half a century, but to many they seemed unlikely partners from the very beginning. Who would have imagined such a marriage? At the time they first met, my mother was a diminutive, shy, fragile-looking ambassador's daughter, sensitive and introspective by nature, a New England intellectual raised in a family widely considered to be both unusually well bred and unusually well read. The Morrows were students, teachers, lawyers, bankers, and diplomats. They valued education above all other opportunities in life, for young women as well as young men, at a time when few Americans attended college at all, and when "bluestocking" was still a common and unflattering term for female scholars. The Morrows had strong family ties, attended the Presbyterian church regularly, and voted, as they served, according to the traditional Republican guidelines of their day. Male and female, Morrows were physically small, but sturdy in constitution and in character, active in society and dedicated to public service.

My father, on the other hand, was a tall, deeply reserved, independent outdoorsman from the Midwest. All his life, he would display a courteous indifference to convention, whether it be intellectual, religious, or political. He rarely attended church, and, to put this quite frankly, he hated school. Only one generation removed from his Swedish immigrant ancestors on the American frontier, my father found his first love, back in the early days of this century, in the Minnesota farm of his boyhood and the natural world extending far beyond it in all directions, into a child's infinity of river and field and forest and wilderness. Above my father's head in those early days, as ever afterward, there stretched the even more compelling infinity of sky.

Then there was my father's father, Charles A. Lindbergh, Sr., known to his contemporaries as C.A. It would be hard to find anyone more different in physique or philosophy from my other, small-statured, large-hearted, conservative banker-diplomat Morrow grandfather than this lanky, outspoken son of Sweden. In his new country, C.A. Lindbergh became a populist congressman who represented Minnesota's progressive Farmer-Labor party. In his speeches the elder Lindbergh routinely decried what he saw as the political machinations and destructive private agendas of "Eastern financiers," men not unlike Dwight W. Morrow, whom he never met. C.A. Lindbergh died three years before his son Charles made the famous flight to Paris, and four years before the goodwill flight to Mexico when the young pilot, Charles A. Lindbergh, Jr., met the ambassador's second daughter, Anne.

My mother often expressed regret that the grandfathers, whom their grandchildren were never to know, had not at least known one another. Her feeling was that the two men were more alike than they were different, despite appearances to the contrary. Once, when she spoke about them, she said, "Your father and I always thought they would have loved each other."

Why not? These two very different grandfathers were both, after all, lifelong public servants, both were dedicated fathers, both were married to strong women with a strong commitment to education. Elizabeth Morrow was a trustee of Smith College, and for a time its interim president, while Evangeline Lindbergh was a high school chemistry teacher.

Whether or not my two grandfathers would have loved each other, two of their children, my parents, Charles Lindbergh and Anne Morrow, loved each other. They flew and wrote and shared a remarkable partnership for many decades, traveling the full length of a tumultuous era of public and private history, side by side. Theirs was a complex and many-layered love story. It was not a simple romance, and it was sometimes an uneasy and uncomfortable union, but my belief, nonetheless, is that neither one of my parents felt fully alive, or truly like himself or herself, unless the other one was there.

Those who research and write about my parents almost always choose to focus on either Charles A. Lindbergh or Anne Morrow Lindbergh, to separate their stories and examine each one individually. It is so easy, in a century that places such value upon individual achievement, to underestimate the power of a partnership, especially in a marriage.

"But this story *is* the marriage," a writer friend observed, and he spoke the truth. Despite their equally independent characters, and their lifelong, separate affinities for solitude—in the air, over the wild places of the earth, or by the sea—my parents' time together marked the most productive period of their lives. After my father's 1927 solo flight brought them together in the first place, all of their most successful ventures were collaborative: the early survey flights; the six children; the many books they wrote, not in collaboration but in mutual awareness, and with mutual support.

We knew, because my father said so, that our mother was the real writer in the family, the Great Writer, however much she might protest. He wrote, too, but he was a flier first, everybody knew that. This made his writing incidental, at least in my mind. His Pulitzer Prize–winning book was about an airplane, naturally enough. The title was the airplane's *name,* for heaven's sake.

For me, my father's writing, like his aerial exploits, fell into the well-ordered, metallic realm of aviation history. It belonged in museums and in textbooks, and had nothing much to do with literature. *The Spirit of St. Louis*, before I actually read it, appealed to me no more than the other books in my father's office: Arnold Toynbee's histories, or Dr. Alexis Carrel's *The Culture of Organs*, or Admiral Jerry Land's *Winning the War with Ships*. (Admiral Land himself, on the other hand, was very appealing. He was a cousin of Uncle's, and had the same blue eyes, but with a flirtatious twinkle in them, and a jaunty naval worldliness that caused me to linger in the living room when he visited.)

And yet a few minutes after I finally sat down to read *The Spirit of St. Louis*, I realized that this book wasn't about an airplane, after all. It was about a boy's relationship to the land, where he grew up, and to the sky, where he came of age. It was about agrarian and technological America coming together in this one boy, my father, through a kind of extension of himself that I recognized in his writing, as I had recognized it on those Saturday afternoons when I had flown with him during my own childhood. It was the story of a thrilling and dangerous adventure and a revolutionary transformation of vision. It was a heroic tale, made to order for a storyteller, and it was told by a master storyteller, with a sense of tension and rhythm and romance and craftsmanship for which I had never given him credit. I discovered for the first time, reading *The Spirit of St. Louis*, that my father was a writer, after all.

I was present at a symposium in 1986 when the writer and historian David McCullough, another Pulitzer Prize–winning author, spoke about his own interest in the prose written by the early aviators, and the fact that so many of these people "proved to be writers of exceptional grace and vision." He later wrote an essay in the *New York Times* about aviator-authors, citing Antoine de Saint-Exupéry, Beryl Markham, and both my parents, and he read aloud the first paragraph of *The Spirit of*

St. Louis. It is one of the most important passages in the book for me; it brings my father back so vividly.

September, 1926

Night already shadows the eastern sky. To my left, low on the horizon, a thin line of cloud is drawing on its evening sheath of black. A moment ago, it was burning red and gold. I look down over the side of my cockpit at the farm lands of central Illinois. Wheat shocks are gone from the fields. Close, parallel lines of the seeder, across a harrowed strip, show where winter planting has begun. A threshing crew on the farm is quitting work for the day. Several men look up and wave as my mail plane roars overhead. Trees and buildings and stacks of grain stand shadowless in the diffused light of evening. In a few minutes it will be dark, and I'm still south of Peoria.

It took my father seventeen years to write the book. Every word was carefully chosen, every word his own. I have heard speculation that my mother may have helped my father in the writing of *The Spirit of St. Louis.* I can confirm that she did. I have heard suggestions that my mother actually wrote some of the book herself, and I can attest that she did not. I don't think she could have, if she'd wanted to, despite my father's dedication, which reads: "To AML, who will never know how much of this book she has written."

Each of my parents, I believe, was the single most important factor in the other's writing career. Nonetheless, they wrote separately, each with a distinct voice. They invariably read one another's manuscripts, and would offer each other suggestions, usually in the form of detailed notes, sometimes page after page of these. Quite often they would sit together in their bedroom with papers spread in piles on the double bed and the door closed, as they went over their notes for hours at a time. A child passing by would hear only a mumble of voices, as one of them read a passage out loud to the other, or a shuffling of papers as a notation was made by one or another, always in pencil.

In our family no comment was ever made in ink on a manuscript, and no note is made, in any medium, on another writer's manuscript. This would be more than discourtesy; it would be a serious violation of personal space.

"These are only suggestions," my father used to say, before he began to read his notes out loud to my mother. My mother would then sigh. I know exactly how she felt. I hate "suggestions," especially from my family, when it comes to my own writing. My father's suggestions usually were logical, based on indisputable facts, but they could be wounding to the sensitivities of a creative artist.

He might say something like this, for instance:

"Let's start by looking at page thirty, paragraph two, where you describe the cloud formations. I made a note here, because in my experience, in a situation following the storm you have described back on page twenty-eight, clouds of this type would not be formed. If you wanted, say, to bring in another weather system entirely, it might be possible to have your cloud shapes, if they are important to you. Now my suggestion . . . and this is only a suggestion . . ."

At this point, if I were the writer whose work was being critiqued, I would be grinding my teeth and mentally cursing all clouds—stratus, cumulus, and nimbus alike—but I could not fault my father's editorial manners. He was unfailingly respectful, if irritatingly accurate. And after all, as an aviator, he did know his clouds.

My mother's suggestions to my father, on the other hand, tended to be stylistic, having to do with commas and hyphens, or with the length of a sentence or a paragraph. I was grateful that she did this for him. I have never been entirely sure what to do with commas myself, but when I was in college I decided that most hyphenated words were unnecessary, even tacky ("star-studded" would be a perfect example). I thought that my father used too many hyphenated words, especially in his environmental writings:

> Walking in the day-long twilight of an Indonesian jungle, I see grotesquely twisting vines of python-width tangle through multi-trunked trees. . . .
>
> "The Wisdom of Wilderness," *Life*, December 22, 1967

I applauded his support of environmental causes, of course, but in 1967 I was a hyphen snob, and to read this sentence made me cringe.

My mother curbed tendencies like this in my father by offering her suggestions gently, with some hesitation. He accepted them without protest, just as I did, whenever I showed her something I had written. We all followed her instincts in these matters. She was the writer in the family . . . the important one.

Although he might edit her book for accuracy, or she might go over one of his essays and point out where it needed cutting, or expansion, or clarity, or fewer hyphens or more commas, I never heard either of my parents question the substance of the other's work, or try to alter the other's voice.

I do know that once, before I was born, my mother tried to change something her husband wrote—the ill-fated isolationist speech he made in Des Moines, Iowa, in 1941, which branded him forever, in some people's eyes, as anti-Semitic. As a child, I knew nothing about this speech. It was another topic nobody talked about, like the flight and the kidnapping, or if they did talk about it, I wasn't listening. When I got to college, though, I found out that the flight and the kidnapping were much less interesting to the other students I met than were my father's prewar activities. Some of my friends confessed that they were surprised to find out that they liked me, considering that my father was a fascist.

Fascist? I was incensed, indignant. What kind of nonsense was this? How could people think such a thing? What did they mean?

"I think you'd better read that Des Moines speech," my closest friend at college said. So I found it, and I read it. I was devastated. I can still feel the sick dizziness that I felt then, bending over the page, reading his words. They were so completely familiar to me, and so alien at the same time, because I understood what he was saying in two different ways. I understood his language because I knew it as well as my own. But I had grown up after the war, and Anne Frank's diary was the book by which I knew the war my father was trying to avoid in 1941. Because of her, I understood the implications my father's words could carry, and did carry for so many people. Reading that speech, I was as angry with him as I have ever been in my life, and I wanted to weep for him at the same time.

It was not that I found a revelation there, some hideous new truth. I did not discover that my father was an anti-Semite, disclosed to me at last as a person whose bigotry and hatred had been somehow hidden throughout the whole of my childhood. I knew that he was not a hater, not a despiser of other people. He was not capable of the ethnic slurs or racial "jokes" I had heard occasionally at the homes of other suburban Connecticut children in the 1950s, those sly, offhand, shriveling remarks that parents made without thinking in front of their children, who never forget them. He would not have been able to laugh at the hopelessly ignorant jokes that the whole country learned, with some effort, to laugh at from Archie Bunker in *All in the Family*. He would have been shocked. I never heard my father talk that way, and I did not find this kind of poison in his speech. I found something else, and I could not forgive him for it.

I was reading with the full, passionate confidence of a college sophomore at Radcliffe in the early 1960s, someone who had not even been alive when the speech was written. All the same, I felt sure that I knew exactly what my father was doing. He was doing what he always did: identifying a situation as he saw it, point by point, and then clarifying it, in his logical way, and then proceeding with his argument in an orderly fashion. The three groups advocating war, he told his 1941 audience, were the British, the Roosevelt administration, and the Jews. He explained why he thought each group took the position it held, and argued that each group was mistaken.

He talked to the American people about isolationism, about the pros and cons of war, about the persecution of Jews in Germany (he spoke before the magnitude of this persecution became known, but I didn't know that then, and I was too horrified to care), the way he talked to his children about Independence and Responsibility, or the Seven Signs of Frostbite, or Punk Design. What was he thinking? How could he have been so insensitive? Was he somebody else in 1941? Did I know my father at all?

"If only he had listened to me," my mother said. "I told him what would happen, if he listed 'Interventionist' groups in that way . . . 'The British,' 'The Roosevelt administration,' and 'The Jews.' I told him he would be called anti-Semitic."

"What did he say?" I demanded.

"He said, 'But I'm not!' "

"And what did you say?"

"I said, 'It doesn't matter. That's what will happen.' But he didn't believe me."

This surprised me. I thought he always believed her. She said that it was different earlier in their marriage. She said that it had been his habit for so long, growing up so alone, to listen only to himself. He had learned to rely on his own judgment, and this had been critical for him, because his survival often depended upon following his instincts. This self-reliance was the reason for the success of his 1927 flight.

"If he had listened to others, he never would have gotten to Paris," she explained. She did not believe that he was anti-Semitic, not even in the isolationist years, not even a little. (I asked her.) But she said that the very qualities that made him a success as an aviator doomed him as a politician. Isolationism, for my father, was a quintessential personal characteristic, my mother believed, and a politically hopeless cause.

This was not to say that she did not support his position, in her own way. In 1940 she published *The Wave of the Future*, a slim tract expressing her own hope for peace, as well as her hopeful sense, at least early on, that fascism in Europe might prove to be a temporary aberration in an ultimately beneficial surge toward European unity, a kind of "scum" soon to be sloughed off and forgotten, on "the wave of the future."

For her hopeful words and her positive outlook, my mother received many letters of support from her readers, although the book had its detractors as well. E. B. White wrote an essay in which he admired my mother's other writings, but characterized her position in *The Wave of the Future* as "a confusion of loyalties." One of her own cousins is said by the family to have retitled the book, in an acid commentary, as *The Undertow of the Past*.

My father told us that *The Wave of the Future* was one of the most beautifully written books he had ever read, and one of the best our mother had ever written.

My mother's editor and close friend, the late Helen Wolff, said to me once that if my father had not died when he did, my mother would have published "another *Gift from the Sea*," a book for women at a later stage in life, containing all the strength and insight of her earlier volume but focusing on a more complex series of issues. Mrs. Wolff told me that she had encouraged my mother, after my father's death, to finish her *Diaries and Letters* series and then work on a collection of essays she was considering, about aging, widowhood, and living alone. My mother finished the volume in the *Diaries and Letters* series that covered my parents' life during the Second World War (*War Within and Without*, Harcourt, 1980), but did not go further with the series or complete any other book after my father died.

I know that she fully intended to write and publish other books during the years that followed their long marriage, because she talked to me about doing this. And yet, it never happened. My own instinct is that she felt, in her sixties and seventies and eighties, that in my father she had lost a professional partner, as well as a personal one. Whether consciously or unconsciously, she was hampered by the feeling that she couldn't complete a book without him. This makes sense to me. After all, she never had.

People generally are much less interested in the partnership my parents shared, or even in the marriage, than in my individual parents. My mother used to laugh about the early years traveling with my father, when her husband was so universally adored that if they stood together in a receiving line, she would resign herself to a long evening of perfunctory handshakes from individuals whose eyes were invariably turned away from hers, and fixed upon the smile of the tall aviator standing beside her.

Then again, I can remember my sister Anne telling me about a gala evening in Washington, D.C., some years ago, when she was presented to her hostess by an eager friend. The friend whispered a little too audibly into the ear of this elegant elderly woman, "She is Charles Lindbergh's daughter, you know." The hostess, exquisitely nurtured blossom of a venerable New England family that she was, smiled at my sister in a gracious, warm, and unhurried manner and at the same time gently, but firmly, corrected the introducer, "You mean, she is *Anne Morrow's* daughter, of course."

There are some differences, admittedly, between the Morrow and the Lindbergh families, and there were certainly differences between my parents as well. But the similarities, and above all the sharings, are more important, I think, in understanding them. I am always amazed, and affectionately amused, when I read *Gift from the Sea,* my mother's most widely loved and in a sense her most characteristic book. I see reflected there, along with her own erudition, eloquence, and craftsmanship, certain unmistakable traces of my father's language, mingled with hers. In the chapter "A Few Shells," for instance, I start to chuckle when she writes about collecting, and then peacefully "selecting" for consideration, shells from the beach as one might, perhaps, "select" and "balance" active and contemplative activities in a more satisfying, less harried life in our modern world.

She speaks of a "natural, not an artificial selection" in her beach life, writes that she will return to her Connecticut home accompanied by the intention to substitute a conscious selectivity based on another set of values . . . involving balance in her physical, intellectual, and spiritual life.

The words "selection" and "balance," repeated by my mother

so many times in this chapter, and in some of her other work as well, are as familiar to me as the nursery rhymes she sang to me in childhood. But unlike the nursery rhymes, these are familiar to me in my father's voice, not my mother's. How many times did I hear those very same words, "selection" and "balance," intoned religiously, over and over, in long, intense living room discussions between my father and my mother and various close friends at the old house in Darien? Hundreds! Maybe more. Then there were the discourses on Darwinian theory that he shared with us, along with thoughtful consideration of "natural selection's" contemporary relevance, or lack thereof. There were many passionate monologues, too, on the increasingly critical need for "balance," between spiritual and scientific values, between the life of the body and the life of the intellect, and between nature and technology, a "balance" that might, if it could be maintained, preserve the wilderness my father had loved as a boy in Minnesota, as well as the wild species of flora and fauna he had grown to love all over the world.

It makes me smile now to realize that *Gift from the Sea*, with all my mother's elegance of style and breadth of wisdom represented in it, and all her literate grace, still brings back vividly to me the voices I used to hear as a child walking down a hallway of my home. This is not the monologue of a single writer, speaking out of isolation. This is the comforting dialogue of parental conversation heard over many years: the thoughts and the theories flowing back and forth; the talking, all the talking, at home and traveling and on walks and at the dinner table, at any hour, in any year, throughout the days of my childhood.

It is moving to find this again and again in my parents' books, now, in my own middle age. Each time the words come fresh from the mind and pen of one parent or the other, and yet each time they are familiar in the old interminglings: my father's words, my mother's voice; my father's voice, my mother's words. This is not just the creative contagion of shared vocabulary, transmitted back and forth between a man and a woman who happen to be writers and who live together. This is something else entirely, something much more powerful than that. It is the living language of a marriage.

I recognize this language most easily when I read what they wrote during the time I was coming of age, in the 1950s and 1960s. When I read my father's "Letter from Lindbergh," for instance, written for *Life* magazine in 1969, I am very much aware of the ways in which my father's thinking in this piece parallel my mother's in *Earth Shine,* a book comprised of two of her essays of the same period: one about the Apollo 8 launching, which she and my father observed together at the John F. Kennedy Space Center in 1968, the other about an earlier trip to East African game preserves in the winter of 1965.

My parents each express a similar concern in these writings, about the changing state of the natural world and about the role of human beings in the fate and future of the earth. I am not sure which of my parents first wrote down his or her thoughts on these matters for publication, nor do I think it is important. Both write about the value of preserving natural environments and of cherishing "wilderness" in the midst of our increasingly technological lives. Both writers also discuss the rapid rate of scientific and technological advancement with a mixture of respect and caution. Both make a plea for greater human awareness, and quietness, and increased human attention to the natural world around us. They had different styles, different audiences, different educational backgrounds, different contexts, but they often had the same thing to say, and said it, each in his or her own way, at the same time.

One becomes very aware, though, reading my mother's first essay from *Earth Shine*, that in writing it she drew upon the profoundly literate tradition of the Morrows. In the second paragraph of her preface, for instance, my mother cites Teilhard de Chardin, Henry Vaughan, John Milton, and Thomas Hardy in one graceful arabesque of argument, saying that human beings have always felt a need to view the world not as citizens of separate nations, but as "terrestrials," citizens of the planet.

The sense of the earth as a whole, as a planet, is with us inescapably. We are unable to forget it or cut it in half in our minds. We think and feel not hemispherically but terrestrially, even though we do not always implement our vision. Teilhard de Chardin once said that he "wanted to express the psychology—the mixed feelings of pride, hope, disappointment, expectation—of the man who sees himself no longer as a Frenchman or a Chinaman but as a Terrestrial." And though there are few men who merit that title as well as he, there have been writers and poets, even before the days of flying, who have spoken as terrestrials. Henry Vaughan, the seventeenth-century poet, "saw eternity the other night/Like a great ring of pure and endless light." In Paradise Lost, Milton envisaged Satan as he "winds with ease/Through the pure marble air his oblique way/Amongst innumerable stars that shone/Stars distant, but nigh-hand seem'd other worlds." Thomas Hardy felt "the roll of the world eastward [as] almost a palpable movement."

The essay on the trip to Africa, too, includes references to Thoreau, Henry Beston, Simone Weil, and the Old Testament, and ends with an affirmation of the creative observation of wildness in nature: "For the act of obeisance to life, wherever one makes it, is in essence religious." It is a remarkably literary piece.

My father, however, when it is his turn, details in a few

boyishly energetic and somewhat startling lines of his "Letter" a whole range of scientific interests that my mother would never have pursued. My father describes these interests, too, in a manner all his own:

Gradually, I diverted hours from aviation into biological research. How mechanical, how mystical was man? Could longevity be extended? Was death an inevitable portion of life's cycle or might physical immortality be achieved through scientific methods? What would be the result of artificially perfusing a head severed from its body?

The difference between the two pieces, both in style and in substance, is clear. What may be less clear, though, is the closeness of the two writers at the time the essays were written. As I read my father's words, I can see him striding through the house in Connecticut, sharing his views with my mother, perhaps even reading the first draft of the *Life* essay aloud to her as he moves around the kitchen, or the living room, or any other place where my mother might be quietly listening to him. She would not ever interrupt, except for an occasional, surprised, almost involuntary interjection at certain points (my guess in this case would be the moment following the sentence about the severed head): "Oh! Charles!"

In some ways my parents were very different. But I have always believed it was their similarities rather than their differences that brought them together and kept them together for so many years: certain shared independencies of character and of spirit that each knew in himself or herself from earliest childhood, and recognized instinctively, immediately, in the other when they first met; certain qualities of solitude and stamina, of reflection and determination. Their mutual recognition must have been profound. This recognition, I think, was

the foundation of the world that they were able to build together for their children. Within that unlikely marriage, over
the difficult years, in spite of the tragedies and the newspapers,
then out of the public eye, and against all odds, my parents
built from their similar characters and shared spirit a family
structure that became the strongest element in their lives. It
remains, I am very sure, the strongest element in mine.

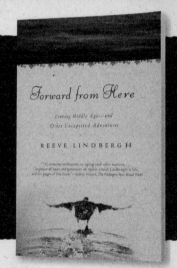